the life *you were* born *to* give

why it's
better to live
than to receive

Published by
THOMAS NELSON
Since 1798
www.thomasnelson.com

Published in Nashville, Tennessee, by Thomas Nelson, Inc.

Thomas Nelson, Inc. books may be purchased in bulk for educational, business, fundraising, or sales promotional use. For information, please e-mail SpecialMarkets@ThomasNelson.com.

Editorial Staff: Debbie Wickwire, acquisitions editor, and Thom Chittom, managing editor
Cover Design: Brandnavigation
Interior Design: Casey Hooper, Book & Graphic Design, Nashville, TN

Library of Congress Cataloging-in-Publication Data

McKinley, David, 1958-
  The life you were born to give : why it's better to live than to receive / by David H. McKinley.
    p. cm.
  Includes bibliographical references and index.
    ISBN-10: 0-8499-1202-4 (alk. paper)
    ISBN-13: 978-0-8499-1202-3 (alk. paper)
  1. Christian life. 2. Generosity. 3. Stewardship, Christian. 4. Bible.
  N.T. Romans--Criticism, interpretation, etc. I. Title.
  BV4501.3.M36 2006
  248.4--dc22

                                                                    2006024019

Printed in the United States of America

07 08 09 10 11 RRD 9 8 7 6 5 4 3 2 1

To Thurman and Mary Hall—
people I never met,
who gave me the greatest gift I have received in life:
my wife.

And to Connie Hall McKinley—
my love, my helpmate, and my best friend.
I love you!

contents

acknowledgments

It is impossible to write a book titled *The Life You Were Born to Give* without giving thanks. The essence of this book offers a vantage point of life from a new perspective. As I see it, this book would not be possible if it were not for the following people:

Tracey Drake, my ministry assistant, works overtime to make projects beyond the daily demands of ministry a possibility. Thank you.

Jennifer Stair has been vital and strategic in my writing to date. She is a superb editor, has outstanding ideas, and is patient to work at my pace. Jennifer, your skill and support provide success. And in God's providence, this is a season of new life for you and Brett. A book and a baby due at the same time—it's like twins! Congratulations.

I appreciate the inspiration, challenge, enthusiasm, and confidence Debbie Wickwire has expressed in me as an author.

The W Publishing Group, led by David Moberg, along with the positive support of Cathy Lewandowski and so many more, have added value to my life and this work. And I appreciate Rhonda Hogan's assistance in detailing my endnotes. Thank you all!

Thank you, Jack and Deb Graham, devoted staff team, and wonderful people called Prestonwood. Your love, encouragement, and support have expanded the platform of my ministry beyond the pulpit to the printed page.

Joseph and Lizzi, you make everything your dad does in life matter more. Thank you.

My prayer is again, and always, "Let this be unto His glory."

foreword

The Life You Were Born to Give is a remarkable book that offers a new perspective on the concept so many of us were raised on—namely, that we should be go-getters. In this book, Dr. David McKinley shares a concept that is far more realistic, encouraging, and scriptural. It's that the *go-givers* are the big winners in life—here and hereafter.

When you observe people who are go-givers, you see joy on their faces and a lilt in their steps. In contrast, go-getters frequently walk around looking like the picture on their driver's license, acting as if somebody licked all the red off their candy! Go-getters continually strive to achieve more and to accumulate more, but they are often not content with their lives, no matter how much "stuff" they have.

When you notice the go-givers, you see an entirely different outlook on life. I recently spoke at the Denton State School, a home for people with mental and emotional problems. The most joyful people were the volunteers who encourage, teach, love, and train the residents to take what God has given them and use it for His glory. Smiles were abundant in that place, and it was a joy to be there!

Several years ago, *Psychology Today* published a study revealing that businesspeople who volunteer to help in the community also do better in the corporate world. These people have discovered that there is joy in serving others because, in most cases, the recipients express appreciation and love to the donors.

As you read *The Life You Were Born to Give*, you will discover how to be the kind of person who is "born to give." You will find insights that will encourage and enable you to enjoy the benefits of the go-giver life. Dr. McKinley's teaching will open your eyes to the delight of knowing your Lord and Savior, as well as the earthly benefits of knowing your heavenly Father. And since I know Dr. McKinley well, having sat under his preaching and teaching for several years, I can testify that he is a man who lives his life to give.

This is a great book, a teaching book, and an encouraging book. It is filled with powerful truths that will inspire you. For that reason, I encourage you to keep a notebook handy as you read. Make notes on what you learn, as well as the incidents that come your way as a direct result of applying what you have learned. Read this book, reflect on it, and then read it again. Use it, and your gratitude bucket will be in overflow position for sure. After all, gratitude is the healthiest of all human emotions—the more you express gratitude for what you have, the more you will have to express gratitude for. Conversely, the more you complain about your problems, the more problems you will have to complain about!

Following the path Dr. McKinley so beautifully describes in this book will enable you, when you get to the goal line of life and look into the end zone, to see the positive impact you have made on your children, grandchildren, and countless friends whose lives you have enriched by applying *The Life You Were Born to Give*. And in the words of the old gospel song, "When we all get to heaven, what a day of rejoicing that will be!"

—ZIG ZIGLAR
Author/Motivational Teacher, Dallas, Texas

introduction
your life is a gift

Remember the words of the Lord Jesus,
that He said, "It is more blessed
to give than to receive."
—ACTS 20:35

Everything we have, we have been given.

Take a moment to consider how your life is connected to other people. Have you consciously reflected on the gifts of time and talent others have given you? As you do, you'll soon realize there are many thank-you notes etched in your heart that are filled with expressions of gratitude for those who have made a difference in you.

Perhaps you had parents who believed in you and sacrificed for your well-being or success. Maybe a teacher encouraged you and inspired you to use your talents for something great. Or it might have been a coach, mentor, colleague, or friend who challenged you and took the time to help you become the person you are today. And then there are pastors, missionaries, Bible study teachers, and authors who helped you see the light and truth by which you now live.

Yet beyond all these supporters who have invested in you, there is a God who made you for Himself. A God who has a purpose for you.

Think about it: your ability to read these words right now is a gift from God. In fact, your very existence is the incredible gift of God, who formed you and gave you life.

Your life is a gift!

1

I love the words of the Psalmist, who said,

You made all the delicate, inner parts of my body
and knit me together in my mother's womb.
Thank you for making me so wonderfully complex!
Your workmanship is marvelous—and how well I know it.
You watched me as I was being formed in utter seclusion,
as I was woven together in the dark of the womb.
You saw me before I was born.
Every day of my life was recorded in your book.
Every moment was laid out
before a single day had passed.
How precious are your thoughts about me, O God!
They are innumerable! (Ps. 139:13–17 NLT)

Our lives were planned for and provided by God. It is by God's providence and provision that we are born to live.

But that's not all. The same God who gave us life is the One who sent His Son, Jesus Christ, into the world to deliver us from condemnation and self-destruction so that we may experience life to the fullest. And this is good news! The God who has given us life now offers us new life—a spiritual transformation according to His purpose and plan.

> **Your life is not your own; it is God's.**

Life—yours and mine—is a gift from God. What we do with our lives is, in many ways, our gift to Him and to the people we touch by His grace. The new nature in Christ involves a new focus of accountability and service. Our lives were not formed for the mere intake of existence. No! To the contrary, we have life—new life in Christ—so that we may understand and discover what it is to "outsource" ourselves for God's glory.

It is now, because of God's grace, that we are born to give.

Your life is not your own; it is God's. He made us to live to give, not live to get. God intends for us to become catalysts for distribution, not containers for consolidation.

When this truth takes root in your mind, it changes your perspective. Taking hold of the reality that you were born to give your life to God fuels every day with a passion for stewardship and service. You begin to understand that what you have, you hold in trust for another.

In Revelation 4:11, we are given a preview of an upcoming picture in heaven. In that day, those gathered around God's throne echo this compelling refrain: "Worthy are You, our Lord and our God, to receive glory and honor and power; for You created all things, and because of Your will they existed, and were created" (NASB). Everything that exists has been created by God and is designed to give glory and honor to God.

In *The Life You Were Born to Give*, we will take a closer look at how we can shift our focus away from getting all we can out of life (existing) to giving our lives away (distributing). Using the book of Romans as our guide, we'll observe and encounter insights for living a life that is, as I like to think of it, "outsourced" for the glory of God. Together, we'll discover that God calls us as believers to come apart from the consumerism and competition of our culture and to become wholly Christlike in our living. Being born to give is a radical, countercultural concept, yet it is thoroughly biblical.

In part 1—"A Life Delivered"—we'll look at our desperate need for God and the grace and redemption provided for us in Jesus Christ, which release us from self-absorbed and self-destructive impulses. In part 2—"A Life Devoted"—we'll explore the essential transition from experiencing God's grace to expressing it to others. And in part 3—"A Life Distributed"—we'll examine practical ways and assorted examples of how we can be set free to live the life we were born to give.

After all, when we receive from God all He has to give, then we discover that the life we were born to live is the life we were born to give.

part 1
a life delivered

Romans 1–11

The objective and substitutionary character of the death of Christ as the supreme demonstration of God's love should result in a transformation of conduct that is effected by the constraining power of that love.

—GEORGE ELDON LADD

He has delivered us from the power of darkness and conveyed us into the kingdom of the Son of His love, in whom we have redemption through His blood, the forgiveness of sins.

—COLOSSIANS 1:13–14

chapter 1
a global system failure

The words SYSTEM FAILURE jumped off the cover in bold, neon yellow letters as I thumbed through an array of weekly news-magazines. I pulled the September 19, 2005, issue of *Time* from the disorderly stack to examine the cover more closely.

The picture depicted the "crash and burn" of a computer shut-down. However, the cover story was not about computers; it was an investigation into the federal government's response to Hurricane Katrina. Photo after photo, tragic scenes were displayed. One by one, people in positions of responsibility were assessed. And page by page, the shame of the fallout was told.

Without a doubt, Katrina not only ravaged the Gulf Coast; it rocked America. Yet for all the physical devastation caused by the massive hurricane, the greatest destruction was the tragic aftermath, which revealed the ugly truth about human nature.

In a special message he preached to his church just weeks after Katrina, Max Lucado aptly describes the scene: "We saw humanity at its best. And we saw humanity at its worst. . . . We are a people of both dignity and depravity. The hurricane blew back more than roofs; it blew the mask off the nature of mankind. The main problem in the world is not Mother Nature, but human nature. Strip away police barricades, blow down the fences, and the real self is revealed. We are barbaric to the core."[1]

Failed expectations. Abuses of power. Undelivered promises. Disrespect for others. Disregard for the law. Every page of the *Time* article revealed the storm and fury lurking in the heart of every man and woman. And what was revealed in the aftermath of Katrina is what the Bible depicts in the aftermath of Adam and Eve.

The Tragedy in the Garden

The story of beginnings, which we read in Genesis, tells of the wonder, honor, and glory of God's creative work on earth. But only three chapters into this story, we read of the devastation caused by a single event that transformed the glory of creation into the shame of human rebellion. It is what theologians refer to as the Fall.

Just days after Hurricane Katrina hit the Louisiana coast, Al Mohler observed that the origins of sin and destruction could be traced all the way back to the book of Genesis. In his daily weblog, he writes, "Genesis three tells the story of the Fall, a story that centers in the volitional, willful act of Adam and Eve to break the command of God, and to do that which the Lord had forbidden. Giving themselves to temptation, they rationalized their desires, justified their action in their own eyes, and ate the fruit that was forbidden them." He goes on to say, "When humans sinned, not only did it affect Adam and Eve and their descendants, but the earth—the cosmos itself—was corrupted."[2]

And so declares the apostle Paul in the book of Romans. The opening chapters of Romans reveal a dark, distasteful, and direct condemnation of mankind in the wake of the storm of sin. The tragedy that occurred in the Garden of Eden resulted in the fallen condition of creation and the complete corruption of the human race.

No One Is Exempt

In Romans 1, Paul describes this global system failure. He declares that the devastating consequences of sin affect the whole world and everyone in it. None can escape the responsibility and results of this global shutdown. No nation. No city. No family. No person.

The *Time* magazine article called four government officials into account for their actions in response to Hurricane Katrina. But Paul calls every person in this world into account when he says, "For the wrath of God is revealed from heaven against all ungodliness and unrighteousness of men, who suppress the truth in

> Life without God is the antithesis of everything we are made for.

unrighteousness, because what may be known of God is manifest in them, for God has shown it to them. For since the creation of the world His invisible attributes are clearly seen, being understood by the things that are made, even His eternal power and Godhead, so that they are without excuse" (Rom. 1:18–20).

And in case we think that somehow we are exempt from this corruption, Paul makes it clear that God's condemnation applies to every member of the human race: "For all have sinned and fall short of the glory of God" (Rom. 3:23).

The fallen state of humanity is the result of a total system failure that had global consequences and personal responsibility. Sin has marred God's design. Sin has captured man's will. Sin has brought judgment upon us all. This is the primary assessment and condition of every culture, of every race, of every person on the planet: "All have sinned and fall short of the glory of God."

To *fall short* means to fail to meet the standard, to fail to attain the goal, to fail to achieve the function for which it was created. Sin has caused a global system failure, and we all need to be delivered from the corrupting power and penalty of this system if we are ever going to truly live the life we were born to give.

Our Only Hope

Life without God is the antithesis of everything we are made for. Therefore, all we have to do is review the assessment of human behavior to understand why our only hope in the aftermath of the Fall is deliverance.

Dr. H. L. Willmington, in his excellent *Guide to the Bible*, describes a scene and presents a "court record" of offenses between "the Supreme Creator of the Universe versus His Sinful Creatures."[3] At the bench of justice, we all stand guilty as charged in the Supreme Court of heaven.

> In the end, the verdict is read: "For all have sinned and fall short of the glory of God" (Rom. 3:23).

Dr. Willmington outlines ten charges presented in a detailed indictment against the human race in Romans 1. God's fierce wrath is revealed against all ungodliness (sins against God's person) and unrighteousness (sins against His will). The "top ten" list is as follows:

1. They held down (suppressed) the truth (1:18).
2. They knew God but did not honor Him as God (1:21).
3. They were unthankful (1:21).
4. They presented foolish speculations (1:21).
5. They allowed their hearts to become darkened (1:21).
6. They thought themselves to be wise but became fools (1:22).
7. They preferred idols to the living God and exchanged His glory for beasts (1:23).
8. They gave their bodies over to sexual perversions (1:26–27).
9. They were filled with unrighteous acts (1:29–32).
10. They knew the seriousness of their crimes but still continued and even encouraged others to join them (1:8–32).

In the end, the verdict is read: "For all have sinned and fall short of the glory of God" (Rom. 3:23). This statement of fact and this verdict of justice is essential if we are to honor the character of God— the Supreme Judge—and escape the terror of our personal judgment.

Listen to how Dr. Willmington describes this scene: "After the Judge has carefully heard all of the evidence and patiently listened to all of the pleas, he finds no other choice but to invoke the supreme penalty, lest true justice be denied. But before the terrible sentence can be carried out, this same Judge quietly closes the case book, lays down the heavenly gavel, rises to his feet, takes off his judicial robes, and goes out to die for the convicted defendants. This and this alone is justification."[4]

Before we can experience the life we were born to live (and ultimately to give), we must first understand our own capture in the system failure of sin. If we cannot be delivered from this failure, we will not fulfill the purpose for which we were created.

For this reason, I close with a final thought from Max Lucado: "When the Katrinas of life blow in, our true nature is revealed and our deepest need is unveiled: a need deeper than food, more permanent than firm levees. We need, not a new system, but a new nature. We need to be changed from the inside out."[5]

I agree. But before we begin our discovery of deliverance, we must go one step further in our discussion of this system failure. We must understand why deliverance will never come through our best efforts to reorganize or rebuild the old system.

the ultimate injustice

Edward Cashman was appointed as a criminal court judge to uphold the laws of the state of Vermont and to protect its citizens. But on January 4, 2006, Judge Cashman handed down a ruling that sent chills down the spines of law enforcement officials and turned the stomachs of parents across the nation. Judge Edward Cashman ruled that Mark Hulett spend sixty days—not sixty years, not sixty months, but only sixty days!—in prison for the repeated rape and molestation of a young girl that started when she was seven and continued over a four-year period.

State prosecutors argued for a minimum eight-year jail sentence. But Cashman, using the full authority of his position on the bench, refused to increase the convicted rapist's jail term, stating, "The one message I want to get through is that anger doesn't resolve anything. It just corrodes your soul."[1]

As I read these words, I was stunned that a judge could find a moralizing basis for tolerance but could not find the moral fortitude to execute the law. It seems to me that this judge traded the responsibility entrusted to him at the bench along with his robes of justice for a counselor's couch and a bully pulpit. And I must admit that from the perspective of a preacher, this was one of the poorest messages I have ever heard.

The problem at the core of this situation was that Cashman was a judge—a trustee of the rights and penalties of the law for the citizens of his community, both families and individuals. Cashman held this trust of law enforcement and judicial responsibility on behalf of the people of Vermont. Yet while this judge was chastising the prosecution and preaching to the victims, what were the physical, emotional, and destructive effects of his actions on the lives of the young girl and her family?

The judge's ruling—or lack thereof—sparked a wildfire of responses so great that the e-mail of Vermont governor Jim Douglas was overloaded and shut down. People across America were shocked and outraged as this story emerged. News talk and legal broadcasts berated and bantered the issue for days. Even Bill O'Reilly took the gloves off as he reviewed the case in his "no spin zone." Gratefully, the governor had the good sense and courage to call for Judge Cashman's resignation.

The overwhelming public pressure and outcry resulted in a change of direction when Cashman finally consented to a three-year sentence before leaving the bench. He said he increased Hulett's sentence only because the state would extend treatment to the known sexual predator while in prison.

Our Innate Sense of Justice

The reason for the passionate furor sparked by the Mark Hulett case is the innate sense of justice we feel when we see such foolish obstruction of law and order in the criminal justice system. We know that such victimization of a child and violation of criminal laws should be met with decisive consequence. But in this case, a judge single-handedly replaced the rule of law with his own personal opinion, and the result was gross injustice.

Without a doubt, the American court system will struggle to survive if judicial opinion replaces law as the basis for civil order. No society can survive if justice is in the eye of the beholder. According to Scripture, that was the condition of life in Israel in the days of the judges, a time when "everyone did what was right in his own eyes" (Judg. 17:6). The result was chaos and corruption. The purpose of the law is to establish an unbiased standard of safety for those who abide and penalty for those who violate.

But for all the harmful, ugly, and distasteful results of injustice we see in our world, there is a far greater picture of injustice in the court of heaven.

God's Radical Injustice: The Guilty Go Free

In Romans 5:8, Paul describes God's judicial system this way: "while we were still sinners, Christ died for us." Here is the ultimate injustice: Jesus, the sinless Son of God, died to pay the penalty of your sin and mine in order that we might be delivered from sin's curse and condemnation and be set free to live the life God intended.

> In God's judicial system, the guilty go free.

In God's judicial system, the guilty go free. This is not because of the failed order or character of the judge, but because of an act of love and grace that fulfilled the highest standard of the law and yet released the most undeserving of sinners: you and me. This seeming injustice—prompted by love—satisfies the highest standard of God's righteousness and allows sinners like you and me to live under the canopy of His mercy and grace.

The apostle Peter understood the mercy of God and the justice of God equally satisfied in Christ. In 1 Peter 3:18, he wrote, "For Christ also suffered once for sins, the just for the unjust, that He might bring us to God, being put to death in the flesh but made alive in the Spirit."

This is the wonder of God's amazing grace. It is the mercy of God in action. Because of Christ and His death on our behalf, we have been forgiven. We are free from the penalty and consequence of the law. God fulfilled justice through the death of Christ. God extended grace and forgiveness through His death to you and to me.

When John Newton—womanizer, slave trader, rebel, and hard-hearted sinner—experienced the divine injustice of God's redemptive grace, he wrote, "Amazing Grace, how sweet the sound, / That saved a wretch like me; / I once was lost, but now am found, / Was blind, but now, I see." This familiar hymn echoes the apostle Paul's refrain as he describes the grace and mercy of God in Romans 5. Jesus has redeemed us from the curse and condemnation of sin. He has delivered us from a system of failure and death. He has empowered us to live in a new dimension.

Here is the core issue of the Christian faith: God does not require us to absolve the guilt of our sin by our efforts to win His approval and fulfill His justice. He accomplished this justice through work of Christ for us. The just died in place of the unjust. And then God extends this forgiveness to us through grace, because Jesus is "just and the justifier" of everyone who believes in His name (Rom. 3:26).

> The new life that God gives us by His grace is all about Christ.

Now life, for those who believe, is all about Christ and His deliverance—His willingness to pay the penalty for our failure in sin and to offer us new life. Paul highlights this truth: "For if when we were enemies we were reconciled to God through the death of His Son, much more, having been reconciled, we shall be saved by His life" (Rom. 5:10).

The new life that God gives us by His grace is all about Christ. The life we now live, we live in Christ and for Christ. We are saved not only by His death, but by His life. We live *in* Christ, and we live *for* Christ.

Through Jesus Christ's willingness by God's grace to taste death, He paid the penalty of our failure in sin and offers us new life. Listen to Paul's description of Christ's work for us: "But the free gift is not like the offense. For if by the one man's offense many died, much more the grace of God and the gift by the grace of the one Man, Jesus

Christ, abounded to many. . . . For if by the one man's offense death reigned through the one, much more those who receive abundance of grace and of the gift of righteousness will reign in life through the One, Jesus Christ" (Rom. 5:15, 17).

What is the sum of it all? Not injustice but justification. Justification is being rendered right. And in this case, sinners like you and me are rendered right with God.

Here's the good news, put plain and simple:

> Death reigned in sin.
> Christ died for us.
> We are justified by faith in our Lord Jesus Christ.

This is incredible! When you receive Christ, this transformational truth becomes reality for you. Our salvation is a wonder of such great proportions that when we understand it, we will never get over it.

> Our salvation is a wonder of such great proportions that when we understand it, we will never get over it.

God condemns us in sin. God provides for us in grace. Jesus dies for us in justice. We are forgiven and made alive through the just and justifying work of Jesus Christ.

When we understand who Christ is and what He has done for us, when we turn from our sin and ourselves in response to God's grace and forgiveness, we receive new life. It is a life of new potential, new power, and new purpose. I can't explain it, but I plan to spend the rest of my life celebrating the wonder of it all.

From Guilt to Grace

Bill and Pam Borinstein had far more than their just reward on earth. Each owning and leading growing companies, they were building track records of proven success. Life for this couple was not one of apparent injustice; it was one of great reward.

But the rewards of success and the enrichment of accomplishment did not leave them with a sense of focus or fulfillment. Instead, all that should have made their lives feel right left them with an aching sense that something was terribly wrong. Building their companies offered them great financial reward, but it left them wondering if their family could survive the stress of their individual and joint success.

A new business venture, a relocation, and a new set of social contacts brought Bill and Pam to Dallas. In the midst of their start-up, someone invited them to a Christmas Eve service at our church. This was a rather curious invitation—one that was outside the lines of conventional thinking for the couple at that time. Bill was a successful, hardworking Jewish businessman, and attending a service at a Baptist church in Texas was not on his radar. Pam was agnostic. She simply had no interest in religious experience, as her own strength and ambition had enabled her to achieve all she wanted in life and more.

Despite their personal religious preferences, the Borinsteins agreed to come to our Christmas Eve candlelight service. There, they experienced something unique in the lives of people who gathered to worship a baby born in a manger more than two thousand years ago. They saw an allegiance and felt an affection in the hearts of those who gathered in that place toward a Jewish carpenter whose business success paled in comparison to the financial empires this couple had established. And as they reflected on the status of their lives and the state of their marriage, Bill and Pam recognized their desperate need for God.

A series of conversations following that Christmas Eve service resulted in a new year of new life for the Borinsteins. They made a discovery that transformed their hearts and their home.

What caused this radical change? Bill and Pam encountered the saving life of Christ.

This couple, who had shared a life of keeping score, encountered the ultimate injustice. Despite all of their success, their lives were overshadowed by the ugly and injurious reality of their human sinfulness. Yet during that candlelight service, they heard the message of the gospel: Jesus came to earth—the just to die for the unjust—so that He might save us from our sins.

Why? Because sin has infected and affected every one of us. We all need a Savior.

For Bill and Pam, their encounter with Jesus Christ changed everything. Overwhelmed by God's mercy and grace, the focus of their lives changed from getting things for themselves to giving away their lives for Christ.

> Sin has infected and affected every one of us. We all need a Savior.

Their change of perspective wasn't motivated by guilt; it was the essence of a captivating grace in their hearts.

And the music of this marriage transformed by Christ echoed John Newton's familiar refrain: "I once was lost, but now am found, / Was blind, but now, I see."

From darkness to light, from guilt to grace, from getting for ourselves to giving our all to Christ—these are the results of experiencing the ultimate injustice demonstrated in the life and death Jesus Christ for us.

Once we have tasted this grace, we will never be the same.

chapter 3
restart for new life

Every time I upgrade my software or install a new program on my computer, I am asked to "restart" in order to enable new functions. I am not required to remove the old programs but rather to allow the new program to overtake and cooperate with my operating system. Restarting my computer allows new capacity while overriding old functionality. After a restart, I can operate in a new realm. Old systems are overridden. New possibilities are released.

This common experience of "restarting" is a great parallel to the insights Paul presents in Romans 6. The principles in this powerful chapter are essential for daily Christian living. As believers, we now have new capacity and functionality because of an internal spiritual restart. Our old operating system (the flesh) can be overridden by the activation of a spiritual software upgrade (new life in Christ).

As Paul Little wrote, "Through Christ we are not only forgiven our individual acts of sin, but we receive a new nature. The Gospel solution is radical, not merely one of outward reform, but inward reform, transforming the heart, the emotions, the will. Someone has said, 'Christ puts a new man in the suit—not just a new suit on the man.' When Christ changes a person, his clothing (his attitudes) will change as well. God has made full provision, through the sacrifice of Christ, for us to escape judgment and have new life."[1]

This new life is lived in the realm of the spirit. It is far superior to the old. While the old is not removed, the new changes everything about our ability to live in the spiritual realm. This upgrade overrides the original, failed system of sin and allows us to access life in a new dimension. We are enabled. We are empowered. We are set free. And we can operate as children of God rather than according to the old desires of the flesh.

> As believers, we now have new capacity and functionality because of an internal spiritual restart.

For this reason, Paul discusses the essential need for every believer to have a spiritual restart. The Spirit of God installs the upgrades and new programs. We must understand, agree, and cooperate by faith as we shut down the old and start up the new. This is the vital life concept we will explore in this chapter. It is a life upgrade made possible by the saving life of Christ.

The Spiritual "Upgrade" Available in Christ

When I was in high school, I came across a book by Major Ian W. Thomas entitled *The Saving Life of Christ*. My spiritual outlook was transformed when I read these words, which helped me understand for the first time that Jesus Christ died not only to forgive my sins and take me to heaven, but also to empower me to live the Christian life today:

> If you will but trust Christ, not only for the death He died in order to redeem you, but also for the life that He lives and waits to live through you, the very next step you take will be a step taken in the very energy and power of God Himself. You will have begun to live a life which is essentially supernatural, yet still clothed with the common humanity of your physical body, and still worked out both in the big and the little things that inevitably make up the lot of a man who, though his heart may be with Christ in heaven, still has his feet firmly planted on the earth. . . . You will be restored to your true humanity—to be the human vehicle of the divine life.[2]

While our redemption has everything to do with life after death, it also has incredible implications for life here and now. We are removed from the penalty of our sin because we are forgiven in Christ. We will be delivered from the presence of sin in heaven. But there is more; we can live beyond the power of sin today! The Christian life is not only future in fulfillment; it is present in empowerment and enablement.

> While our redemption has everything to do with life after death, it also has incredible implications for life here and now.

This is what Paul declares in Romans 6:1–4: "What should we say then? Should we continue in sin in order that grace may multiply? Absolutely not! How can we who died to sin still live in it? Or are you unaware that all of us who were baptized into Christ Jesus were baptized into His death? Therefore we were buried with Him by baptism into death, in order that, just as Christ was raised from the dead by the glory of the Father, so we too may walk in a new way of life" (HCSB).

In Christ, we are given a new way of life. We are no longer limited and enslaved to the old system. We have an upgraded system of power available to us. Where did it come from? When did we get it? How do we experience it? These are the questions Paul addresses throughout this chapter.

Reading Romans 6 is like reading a description of the latest version of software. It parallels the old life and the new life, and it highlights the change we can experience and enjoy. Let's examine this concept further.

A Picture—United with Christ in Baptism

In the opening words of Romans 6, Paul uses the term "baptism" to describe Christ's work on our behalf. The concept of baptism is used two ways in the Bible, so let's look at both.

First, baptism is used in Scripture to describe the inward and eternal work of the Holy Spirit, effective in our lives at the moment of salvation. We cannot separate the work of Christ and of the Holy Spirit. Scripture declares, "For by one Spirit we were all baptized into one body—whether Jews or Greeks, whether slaves or free—and have all been made to drink into one spirit" (1 Cor. 12:13). This baptism of the Holy Spirit is enacted at the moment of our salvation. Paul goes on to say, "But you are not in the flesh but in the Spirit, if indeed the Spirit of God dwells in you. Now if anyone does not have the Spirit of Christ, he is not His" (Rom. 8:9).

> Baptism is a picture of our union with and surrender to Christ so that we no longer live for ourselves. Our life is all about Him.

The baptism of the Holy Spirit is not a secondary work after salvation. It is the very work of the Spirit in the event of salvation itself, whereby we receive new life in Christ. Paul emphasizes this new life when he writes, "Therefore we are buried with Him through baptism into death, that just as Christ was raised from the dead by the glory of the Father, even so we also should walk in newness in life. For if we are united together in the likeness of His death, certainly we also shall be in the likeness of His resurrection" (Rom. 6:4–5).

On another level, baptism is also used in the Bible to describe the physical act of immersion into water as a witness and testimony of Christ. This act of publicly identifying ourselves as followers of Christ is important for Christian obedience. Jesus included it specifically in His final words to His disciples in Matthew 28:19–20: "Go therefore and make disciples of all the nations, *baptizing them* in the name of the Father and of the Son and of the Holy Spirit, teaching them to observe all things that I have commanded you" (emphasis added). All believers are to be baptized in order that they may declare their personal salvation and surrender to Christ.

When you call upon the name of the Lord Jesus Christ and are saved (see Rom. 10:9–10), the first command you are to obey is baptism. Why? Because baptism identifies you with the death, burial, and resurrection of Christ. You must surrender your body to go underwater. Through this surrender, you proclaim Christ through a picture without words. The person you were before Christ you are no more. You are buried with Christ in the likeness of His death. You are dead to your old life and its sin, and you are raised to walk in newness with Christ. Your life is not your own. You belong to Christ.

In many ways, baptism for a Christian is like a wedding ring for a married person. You don't have to have a ring to be married, but your wedding ring is an outward sign to everyone that you belong to another. Something has happened in your heart that you want to declare and be associated with every day of your life.

If you read the Gospels, you will discover that Jesus's first act in His public ministry was being baptized by John in the Jordan River. Before Jesus healed the sick, taught the Beatitudes, or walked on water, He was baptized by John.

Have you ever asked yourself, "Why was Jesus baptized?" Did He need to repent of sin? No. Did He do it in order to become the Savior? Of course not. The heavens opened to declare, "This is My beloved Son, in whom I am well pleased. Hear Him!" (Matt. 17:5). So why was He baptized?

Jesus was baptized at the outset of His public ministry to declare and demonstrate to others what He came to do for us. Jesus publicly identified with us in baptism. By surrendering His body to go under the water and then being raised up from the water, He pictured His work on our behalf through His death, burial, and resurrection. Jesus identified with us and commanded that we be identified with Him. Baptism is a picture of our union with and surrender to Christ so that we no longer live for ourselves. Our life is all about Him.

But there is more for us to understand. Paul moves from the picture of baptism to a presentation of the spiritual restart necessary in the life of every believer.

A Presentation—Dead to Sin but Alive to God

We often associate a presentation with a lecture or demonstration that we need to attend, listen to, and observe. However, Paul calls us to a presentation of a different kind. It is one where you understand, respond, and release. What is pictured in baptism is now to be practiced in daily life: "knowing this, that our old man was crucified with Him, that the body of sin might be done away with [literally, rendered inoperative], that we should no longer be slaves of sin" (Rom. 6:6).

> Because of our relationship with Christ, we no longer have to serve the old life.

This is strong and graphic language. Everybody serves somebody. It may be yourself. It may be your stuff. It may be your boss, your job, or your ambition. Paul's point is clear: we all used to be enslaved to the flesh, but because of our relationship with Christ, we no longer have to serve the old life.

Then Paul describes a new program, uploaded in our lives by the Spirit of God and accessible to every believer. "Likewise you also, reckon yourselves to be dead indeed to sin, but alive to God in Christ Jesus our Lord. . . . And do not present your members as instruments of unrighteousness to sin, but present yourselves to God as being alive from the dead, and your members *as* instruments of righteousness to God. For sin shall not have dominion over you, for you are not under law but under grace" (Rom. 6:11, 13–14).

I love the way *The Message* translates verse 11: "From now on, think of it this way: Sin speaks a dead language that means nothing to you; God speaks your mother tongue, and you hang on every word. You are dead to sin and alive to God. That's what Jesus did."

In other words, we now live in Christ with His power, for His purpose, and for His glory. Our life is not ours; we belong to Christ. We must "restart" spiritually—not resolve, reform, or renew, but restart—

by grace through faith and begin living in the realm of new capacity in Christ.

This is the core of Christianity. As believers, we are not aligned with a code, enlightened through education, or rehabilitated through effort. We are empowered to live a new life in Christ. In the book of Colossians, Paul put it like this: the ultimate reality is "Christ in you, the hope of glory" (1:27).

Once we understand this concept of presentation, it changes our priorities and practices. We no longer indulge ourselves according to the flesh. We are now empowered and enabled to live in the new dimension of grace.

A Practice—Yield Yourself to God

Instead of living in the virus-ridden limitations of the old software, we are called to experience and enjoy the upgrade available to us in Christ. When we discover the power Christ has given us, we are finally free to experience the new life—the life we were born to give.

Paul states, "Do not continue offering or yielding your bodily members [and faculties] to sin as instruments (tools) of wickedness. But offer and yield yourselves to God as though you have been raised from the dead to [perpetual] life, and your bodily members [and faculties] to God, presenting them as implements of righteousness" (Rom. 6:13

> When we discover the power Christ has given us, we are finally free to experience the new life—the life we were born to give.

AMP). In other words, we should not continue the old program. Instead, we are to activate and experience the full operation of our "restart" into a new system.

I come back one last time to Major Ian W. Thomas, who says, "There is something more which makes Christianity more than a reli-

gion, more than an ethic, and more than the idle dream of the senti-
mental idealist. It is this something that makes it relevant to each one
of us right now as a contemporary experience. It is the fact that Christ
Himself is the very life content of the Christian faith. It is He who
makes you 'tick.' . . . He is Himself the very dynamic of all His
demands."[3]

In January 2006, Apple Computer founder and president Stephen
Jobs announced a new dynamic in the Mac computer. Macs have
long been known for their incredible capacity and functionality. But
now Intel, the microchip that has long been associated with PCs, has
become a partner and component in the Mac. Commercials promot-
ing the new product declare, "For years, the Intel chip was limited to
little boxes performing repeat functions; but today, there's a world of
new possibilities."

So it is when we discover the saving life of Christ. When we
embrace the restart concept of Romans 6, we experience a world of
new possibilities. We not only live the life we were born to live, but
begin to discover the life we were born to give.

chapter 4
the firewall of God's love

All across America, people celebrate Independence Day with community gatherings and barbecues, parades, picnics, hot dogs, ice cream, watermelon, and, of course, fireworks. These are the mainstays for most of us on the Fourth of July.

Not long ago, my Fourth of July started with a bark, not a bang. Connie and I were walking our Labrador retriever, Lilly, just before 7 a.m. when we heard a male voice echoing through the streets about a block away from our path, "Lucky, Lucky, LUCKY! Come here, boy!" I looked around, expecting to see a runaway dog charging around the corner.

Within minutes, the man appeared on a bicycle. No shirt. No shoes. Just shorts. He asked us if we had seen a small, fluffy dog named Lucky. "No, we haven't," I said, "but we'll keep our eyes open." He told us that their dog had escaped from the backyard, and his wife and kids were devastated.

As the man started to pedal away, he looked back at us and said, "There's a one-thousand-dollar reward for anyone who finds that dog."

We kept walking. Connie and I thought about the fear and pain of losing a family pet. We thought about children's tears, a mother's frustration, and a father who was doing all he could to find their beloved family pet.

I prayed, "Lord, let us help this man and his family." The church I served as pastor was just a few blocks away, and I thought this could be a great opportunity to reach out to his family.

We turned the corner and continued our walk on a path that went through thick stands of Banyan trees. In Florida, where we lived at the time, these trees grow to enormous size and density. As we cleared the trees, we spied a small, white dog. While I held back our excited Lab, Connie cautiously approached the small dog and gently called, "Lucky!"

Slowly but surely, Lucky made his way to Connie. She snagged him by the collar and picked him up. We were going to be heroes on this Fourth of July morning!

About a block ahead, I saw the man ride across the street, still calling Lucky's name at the top of his lungs. I waved at him and pointed at Connie, who was holding the furry bundle. When he saw us, he started racing down the street, shouting, "Come here, Lucky! Come!"

Connie let go of Lucky at the man's request, and the dog ran right past him. The man turned and jumped off the bike. Thankfully, Lucky knew his way home, and the man gave chase all the way down the street to his front yard. Finally, a reunion!

I handed our dog's leash to Connie, picked up the man's bike, and followed him back to his house. He was out of breath from the chase and reached out his hand to say thanks. Just then, I felt something pressed into my hand. I looked down and saw a stack of crisp one-hundred-dollar bills. I told him I had no intention of taking any money. We were overjoyed to help him find his dog.

When he refused my effort to return the money, I said, "Please, I am the pastor of the church on 4th Avenue. I would be honored just to have you and your family come and hear me speak." He replied, "We may, but thanks," and ran up the steps to his house.

I didn't know what to do. Here I was, taking a routine walk with my wife around our neighborhood one Saturday morning, when a momentary encounter resulted in a man handing me a reward for finding his dog.

I started counting. "One, two, three . . ." There were ten one-hundred-dollar bills—a thousand bucks! Talk about fireworks. My emotions were exploding. I felt great and terrible at the same time. I didn't want any money; I just wanted to help someone in need. Now I was wondering if I could safely make it back to the house without a holdup!

As we walked along, I handed the money to Connie. "You are the one with the dog magic," I said. She smiled but refused. "Please take it and do something for yourself," I urged. She would have none of it. As we finished our walk, we discussed what we should do with the money.

When we arrived home, I told our kids about the encounter. I wish I had a photo of their faces as I counted the money and laid it on the table. They were dumbfounded, just like their dad. What were we going to do with so much money?

> The love of God is a firewall of security and protection against all elements of disruption and invasion in life.

Now lest you forget, I am a pastor. Everything in my life is a potential sermon illustration. So the next morning, as I shared a message that focused on the depth and wonder of God's love for us, I told the story about Lucky. I held up the ten one-hundred-dollar bills, and then I put them in the offering plate. I told the church it was not mine yesterday, and I didn't deserve it today. But Connie and I could give the money as an expression of our gratitude for God's grace and love. It was all we could do.

The Depth of God's Love

The apostle Paul described the incredible dimensions of God's love in Romans 8. He wants us all to know that the love of God is a firewall of security and protection against all elements of disruption and invasion in life. Let's pause to consider this concept.

What can we say about such wonderful things as these? If God is for us, who can ever be against us? Since God did not spare even his own Son but gave him up for us all, won't God, who gave us Christ, also give us everything else? Who dares accuse us whom God has chosen for his own? Will God? No! He is the one who has given us right standing with himself. Who then will condemn us? Will Christ Jesus? No, for he is the one who died for us and was raised to life for us and is sitting at the place of highest honor next to God, pleading for us.

Can anything ever separate us from Christ's love? Does it mean he no longer loves us if we have trouble or calamity, or are persecuted, or are hungry or cold or in danger or threatened with death? (Even the Scriptures say, "For your sake we are killed every day; we are being slaughtered like sheep.") No, despite all these things, overwhelming victory is ours through Christ, who loved us.

And I am convinced that nothing can ever separate us from his love. Death can't, and life can't. The angels can't, and the demons can't. Our fears for today, our worries about tomorrow, and even the powers of hell can't keep God's love away. Whether we are high above the sky or in the deepest ocean, nothing in all creation will ever be able to separate us from the love of God that is revealed in Christ Jesus our Lord. (Rom. 8:31–39 NLT)

The God who created us is the God who redeemed us. We cannot begin to imagine the depth of His love for us.

As I saw a father pass through neighborhood streets calling out for his dog, I thought of the God of heaven, who took on human flesh and stepped into His creation to call us back to Himself. And He paid not a reward but the ransom of sin and death so that we can know the joy, peace, and life made possible by His grace.

The grace of God is the only means whereby we can be saved. It is all of God and none of me. God saw our lost and helpless condition and sent His own Son to fulfill the "righteous requirement of the law" in order that we might be forgiven and set free from condemnation and a life of corruption (see Rom. 8:3–4).

And because salvation is all God's doing, by grace, we are kept now and forever in His love. We cannot maintain our salvation by our own efforts any more than we could achieve, acquire, or earn our salvation by our own efforts. The everlasting security of our faith is God's unfailing and unconditional love for us.

Through Christ, we can live a new life. Not the life of achievement according to the flesh but the new life of indebtedness to grace.

Eugene Peterson does a masterful job of giving expression to Paul's words in Romans 8:12: "So don't you see that we don't owe this old do-it-yourself life one red cent. There's nothing in it for us, nothing at all. The best thing to do is give it a decent burial and get on with your new life. God's Spirit beckons. There are things to do and places to go!" (MSG).

> The new life is all about living out an obligation to grace. It is the life we are born to give.

Do you see it? The new life is all about living out an obligation to grace. It is the life we are born to give. And we give our life in devotion and service to Christ, not to earn our salvation or to achieve a sufficient measure of grace, but because our life has been swallowed up in the grace, mercy, and love of God.

Secure in Christ

The best part of the whole picture is this: we are secure in Christ. We are free from the condemnation of sin. God's love provides a firewall against condemnation, accusation, and judgment. Our salvation is a current, present, real-time experience for us. Our faith and forgiveness are secure because they are based on what God did through His Son, by grace.

We are no longer condemned by our sin, but we are freely accepted in Christ (Rom. 8:1). We are adopted into God's family and are now children of God (Rom. 8:14). Whatever life brings, whenever life stings, and wherever life leads, we are sure of His grace and secure in His love. He is working *in* us, He is working *for* us, and He is working *through* us for His glory (Rom. 8:28).

> We stand in grace, and we are held by love.

The apostle Paul concludes Romans 8 with a convincing argument about God's unfailing love. Nothing can ever separate us from His love. Everything He has done is an expression of the marvelous grace and infinite love of the Father toward us.

We are not lucky; we are sure.

We stand in grace, and we are held by love.

My brief encounter with a dog named Lucky was more than an experience to remember; it was a lesson to remind all of us that God's love is not measured by our worth but by His amazing grace.

chapter 5
time to rethink everything

Stephen Covey's *The 7 Habits of Highly Effective People* is one of the best-selling self-help books of all time. But there is a lesser known book on the shelf at my house entitled *The 77 Habits of Highly Ineffective Christians*. It's a cynic's adaptation of a great work, and it's brilliant.

Chris Fabry approaches the subject of ineffective Christianity in an unorthodox fashion. He provides the reader with a clue to his satiric style in the very beginning of the book. On the page where you would expect to find acknowledgments, you read instead, "An ineffective Christian never remembers to thank anyone under any circumstances. Might as well learn that before you read this book."[1]

The seventy-seven habits of ineffective Christians that Fabry discusses in this book include:

• Habit #1: Dichotomize Your Life

• Habit #6: Base Your Faith Solely on Feelings and Experience

• Habit #13: Be Thankless

• Habit #23: Cultivate Worry

• Habit #51: Become a Walking Cliché

But the habit that relates to our discussion here is "Habit #12: Be a Spiritual Sponge." Fabry describes this highly ineffective but all too common Christian habit like this:

Spiritual sponges show up at every service, take notes on ser-
mons, memorize verses, attend retreats, buy Christian books
galore and subscribe to every Christian magazine and devotional.

Spiritual sponges know all the kings of the Old Testament.
In alphabetical order. Spiritual sponges know the diet of the
prophets, how many calories are in a locust and how much the
ark would cost today if built with the original materials. Spiritual
sponges desire the true trivia of the Word.

Unlike "hearers," spiritual sponges are open to correction and
will change sinful habits and behaviors in their lives. What spiritual sponges do not do is use their knowledge to help others.
They will not teach a class. They will not present themselves for
leadership in the church. They won't drive a bus or take the
offering, and most of all, they will not engage anyone outside the
church in meaningful conversation regarding what they know.

Call them shy, call them intellectual, call them introspective.
Just don't call on them to pray out loud during a service. If you
must learn more about the Bible and the Christian life, make
sure you imitate the spiritual sponge, and you will be filled with
lots of knowledge but empty of concern for others.[2]

Before Christ, life is all about getting. In Christ, life is all about
giving. Why? Because there is a metamorphosis in the heart, mind,
and will. We understand that all we are and all we have are given to
us. And this is the all-encompassing truth Paul presents as the pre-
lude to the second portion of the book of Romans.

To God Be the Glory

Having reviewed and examined in the first eleven chapters of
Romans what God has done for us by grace, Paul now prepares to
challenge our response. But before he issues a call to action, Paul
brings his insight and instruction to a climactic confession in the

closing verses of Romans 11: "Oh, the depth of the riches of the wisdom and knowledge of God! How unsearchable his judgments, and his paths beyond tracing out! 'Who has known the mind of the Lord? Or who has been his counselor? Who has ever given to God, that God should repay him?' For from him and through him and to him are all things. To him be the glory forever! Amen" (vv. 33–36 NIV).

Did you catch the last verse? It all comes down to this: all things are *from* God and *through* God and *to* God.

Life is not about us; it is all about God and His glory.

Paul makes this confession in the context of having reviewed God's covenant with Israel and their response (or lack thereof). But the point of Romans 9 to 11 is clear: life is all about God. Everything God has done in history—including His redemption provided in Jesus Christ—is for His glory.

Everything is for God's glory. Therefore, the life we have been born to live, we are born to give for His glory!

In Romans 11:36, Paul preaches a message with three points. Here are the three main points the apostle Paul wants to impress in our hearts:

- God is the Source of everything ("of Him")
- God is the Sustainer of everything ("through Him")
- God is the Sum of everything ("to Him")

When we embrace this God-centered view of life, we experience a radical change in our perspective. We realize that life is not about us; it's about God. The life we are born to live is the life we are born to give for the glory and pleasure of God.

Seeing Ourselves As God's Stewards

When we experience the reality of the life we were born to give, our response is to see our life as a stewardship. We are stewards of the life God has given us.

What do I mean by stewardship? Let's explore this concept together. As a pastor, I am keenly aware that the word *stewardship* tends to find only one application in the Christian community—money. When we hear *stewardship*, we often think *fundraising*. But a biblical understanding of life stewardship will transform a person who has made a profession of faith into a fully devoted follower of Jesus Christ.

The Greek word often translated "steward" in the Bible refers to a person who was responsible for the administration of a household and all of its contents. Stewards were managers of the property. They did not own the property for themselves, but they managed and administrated the daily functions of that property and household in accordance with the will of the owner.

A steward is one who has been charged with the authority and responsibility to act on behalf of another. In other words, the focus of a steward's life is to attend to the tasks and concerns of the owner. And he is accountable to the owner for his stewardship and faithfulness.[3]

That's it! Life isn't about us; it's about God. It is all about the Owner and our responsibility to Him. Our body? It's His property. Our time? It's His resource. Our bank account? He's providing the allowance. It's all about God. Everything!

Everything we have, we have been given.

When we recognize that all we are, all we have, all we enjoy, all we face, all we want, and all we need is found in relationship to the One who owns our dwelling and everything in it, then our life is one of devotion to Him and Him alone.

The Compelling Motive of Stewardship

We are not called to be spiritual sponges. Sponges soak, sit, and sour. We are called to be stewards. We live to give, serve, and honor the Master of our house.

Stewardship is the compelling motive and defining perspective of authentic Christian living. Because we are grateful to God for His great mercy toward us and because we desire to honor Him in every part of our life, we want to be faithful stewards. When we realize that all we have been given we hold as a trust for another, our focus becomes not one of ownership, but rather of stewardship of the life we have been given for God's glory.

This understanding of stewardship will revolutionize how our faith is translated into the details of daily life. When stewardship becomes our focus, everything in our life is affected by this reality. We are not our own; we belong to God. All we have is His. He has called us and enabled us to live as a steward of His grace and mercy in our life. We will, by His grace, live for God's glory.

> We are called to be stewards. We live to give, serve, and honor the Master of our house.

In his book *Stewardship: Total Life Commitment*, R. Leonard Carroll provides an expanded perspective of stewardship through scriptural characters, teachings, and experiences. While Dr. Carroll and I come from different backgrounds theologically and spiritually, this book is one of a kind on the subject of stewardship. I have found his insights to be of great benefit in my own research and reflection.

In summary, Dr. Carroll says, "Stewardship is the recognition that 'all' of life and possessions are gifts of God to be used for the strengthening of the individual life and for extending the kingdom of God. Practical stewardship transformed the apostolic church and gave it power which made it triumphant. Total-life commitment is still the focal point for more and better Christian living!"[4]

A fuller discovery of how our new life in Christ is based on the principle of stewardship will revolutionize our walk with Christ. It will call for devoted hearts and a deeper understanding of why we have been "delivered . . . from the power of darkness and conveyed . . . into the kingdom of the Son of His love" (Col. 1:13). Most of all, it will empower you to live a life that is distributed for the glory of God.

Now it's time to take a fresh look at life and to rethink everything.

a life delivered

Before we move forward on our journey of discovery concerning the life we were born to give, we must pause to consider where we are in relationship to the realities of life we have reviewed in Romans.

Without Christ, we are without life. For this reason, we must be "born again" to live the life God has planned and provided through Jesus Christ. This life begins when we are "born again" and begin to walk in the "newness of life" found in Christ. It is necessary for each of us to know and experience the deliverance and life transformation that comes from Christ and Christ alone.

Have you experienced God's deliverance in your life?

The Problem We All Face

"For all have sinned and fall short of the glory of God" (Rom. 3:23).

Sin is a universal virus that has separated every one of us from God's plan and purpose for our lives. We cannot make excuses, blame others, or escape the reality of sin and its consequence in each of our lives.

The Penalty We Cannot Escape

"For the wages of sin is death, but the gift of God is eternal life in Christ Jesus our Lord" (Rom. 6:23).

God's justice demands satisfaction. But we cannot reconnect ourselves or overcome the damaging impact of sin by our own strength. For this reason, Jesus came into the world and experienced injustice so that we might be made just and right and have good standing before God. Apart from Jesus, we have no hope of deliverance from the penalty of sin.

The Passion That Changes Everything

"But God demonstrates His own love toward us, in that while we were still sinners, Christ died for us" (Rom. 5:8).

God loves you and has provided a way for you to know and experience His power and purpose for your life. The wonder of God's love and the reach of His grace are seen in the passion of Christ opening the door for new life to all who believe on His name.

The Promise That Calls for Response

"If you confess with your mouth the Lord Jesus and believe in your heart that God has raised Him from the dead, you will be saved. For with the heart one believes unto righteousness, and with the mouth confession is made unto salvation. For 'whoever calls on the name of the LORD shall be saved'" (Rom. 10:9–10, 13).

Come to God—just as you are, today—and experience the life Jesus gives. And when you do, you will understand and embrace this truth: the life you are born to live is the life you are born to give.

part 2
a life devoted

Romans 12:1–2

If Jesus Christ be God, and died for me, then no sacrifice can be too great to make for Him.

—C. T. STUDD

I appeal to you therefore, brothers, by the mercies of God, to present your bodies as a living sacrifice, holy and acceptable to God, which is your spiritual worship. Do not be conformed to this world, but be transformed by the renewal of your mind, that by testing you may discern what is the will of God, what is good and acceptable and perfect.

—ROMANS 12:1–2 ESV

chapter 6
a change of heart

I spent five days in Panama, but I never saw the Panama Canal. It is amazing how close you can be to something so magnificent and miss it entirely.

I did, however, make a discovery while I was in Panama that I will never forget. One cold January morning, I boarded a flight to Panama with my son, Joseph, as part of a group to distribute Christmas shoeboxes through the annual Operation Christmas Child outreach of Samaritan's Purse. Though our family had prepared shoeboxes for this outreach for more than a decade, this year my son and I would personally deliver several thousand of those boxes to needy children in some of the remote areas of Panama.

Our first distribution was in a children's hospital in David City. I will never forget the expressions on those young faces as we distributed shoeboxes filled with small toys, school supplies, and other gifts. The room was filled with smiles, tears, and laughter. This incredible experience was forever etched in my heart.

We made our way from the city to several smaller villages a half-day's drive away. Again, we saw hundreds of children gather as pastors and missionaries shared a shoebox of gifts and a message of hope with each child who came.

On our last day of distribution, our group gathered with a church under an open-air pavilion. We watched as children and families came from lean-to shelters over the hills above us and made their way along footpaths to the gathering for the shoebox distribution.

Joseph and his friend Ty Robinson brought a word of greeting to all who gathered. We stood by the mounds of shoeboxes and distributed them one by one to the children as they made their way to the area where we were standing.

As we were nearing the end of our time, a young man named Alex approached us. He was fourteen, and regrettably, we had no boxes left for boys his age. Though we often had an abundance of boxes for smaller children, we were pressed to meet the need for kids between the ages of ten and fourteen.

Through an interpreter, I learned that Alex was a fan of the Dallas Cowboys. How I wished for a gift with a big Texas star! I also learned he was a Christian, and I told him that we were brothers in Christ. Then I introduced him to Joseph. They spent some time talking, and I could tell Joseph really made a connection with Alex.

When Alex started up the hill toward his home, I wondered what the future would hold for this young man. He was so bright and pleasant. Yet in his village, with limited life support and resources, what could he hope to do in life?

After traveling partway up the hill, Alex turned around and came running back toward us. He motioned for an interpreter and said, "Thank you for coming. I hope you have a great trip and, if not here, I will see you in heaven." Wow! What a powerful moment. We praised God for the joy and confidence in our common faith. We shook hands, gave high fives, and he left. I knew that my son and I would never forget Alex.

I had no idea how my brief acquaintance with Alex would impact my heart.

The "Panama Canal" of Our Faith

Panama is the hinge of North and South America and the gateway between the Caribbean Sea and Pacific Ocean. The Panama Canal, built by the United States in the early 1900s, is an engineering marvel and a sailor's dream. This canal transformed the shipping and commerce of the world.

Just as the Panama Canal provides connection, transition, and transformation in the shipping world, there is a point of passage in the book of Romans that changes the entire dynamic of our faith in life. It is Romans 12:1–2. These two verses are the "Panama Canal" of the Christian faith, linking the deep blue waters of doctrine with the clear waters of daily Christian living.

In Romans 12:1–2, the apostle Paul writes, "I beseech you therefore, brethren, by the mercies of God, that you present your bodies a living sacrifice, holy, acceptable to God, which is your reasonable service. And do not be conformed to this world, but be transformed by the renewing of your mind that you may prove what is that good and acceptable and perfect will of God."

> Romans 12:1–2 is the passage that moves us from getting right with God to living right for Him and with others.

There is a distinct transition between the foundational theology of Romans 1–11 and the practical instruction of Romans 12–16. But Romans 12:1–2 is the hinge. It is here that truth and life, faith and works, substance and evidence meet. Romans 12:1–2 is the passage that moves us from getting right with God to living right for Him and with others.

As Dr. Adrian Rogers used to say, "Whenever the Bible provides a *therefore*, we must pause and see what it is *there for*." My study of Romans 12:1–2 has led me to believe that the "therefore" of this passage is not a single connection to the end of chapter 11, but rather a canal connecting the first eleven chapters to the practical and instructional chapters that follow. In other words, everything God has done for us is the groundwork for all God wants to do in and through our lives today.

Romans 12:1–2 is a call to respond to God's mercy from the heart. It is a call to measure all God has done and to let the ocean of God's love and grace flow into the sea of Christian service and living.

When this happens, we are changed forever. Mercy does that. It overwhelms us with gratitude and calls us to devotion. Nothing unites hearts like the flow of mercy. And the Christian life is a response to the mercy of God.

Now I am not implying that Christianity is merely emotion or sentiment. But I believe that God's greatest desire is the total devotion of our hearts in response to the wonder of His great mercy and grace. God knows that when He has our hearts, He will have our minds.

> Our ambition is to live in response to God's mercy measured in our life.

Many try to live for Christ merely from the head. That is, they learn, choose, decide, and commit according to their understanding of biblical teaching. Now don't misunderstand me: knowledge of the truth is essential for effective Christian living. Why else do you think God provided a written record of revelation and truth? But the Christian life is much more than human reasoning grounded in divine truth. It is a daily response to God's mercy and grace. It is a change of heart that connects with everything else in life. As the hymn writer so eloquently expressed, "Love so amazing, so divine, / Demands my life, my soul, my all!"

Our ambition is to live in response to God's mercy measured in our life. Therefore the only thing that makes sense is for us to present our bodies as living sacrifices to Him by saying, "Here we are, Lord; we are totally devoted to you."

Our desire is not to get but to give. The life we are born to live in Christ is now the life we are born to give for Christ.

An Emblem of Mercy

This is the most essential reality in the Bible: we live in faith and response to the God who has loved us, redeemed us, and called us into relationship with Him. All of life becomes a thank-you for God's goodness and grace extended to us.

That is what took me to Panama. It was my heart's desire to share with others because of the magnificent mercy God has measured to me. This is the only reasonable response to God's mercy in our lives. All we want to do, day by day, is to live with a view of gratitude for all God has done for us.

I thought about the wonder of God's goodness and love as our van pulled away from the village where Alex lived. People from all over the community, arms loaded with gifts, stood along the street, which was lined with remnants of wrapping paper. Their waves and smiles are etched in my memory even today.

But that wasn't the end of the story. Joseph and I returned home to our familiar environs of life in Texas. It was January, and the adventure of a new year had just begun. It was a year that would be defining in many ways. In May, Joseph graduated from high school. In June, my mom stepped into heaven. In August, Joseph started college in Virginia. It was a year of highs and lows, a year of new beginnings and bittersweet endings. As a family, we shared some wonderful and tender times. And there is one moment I must share with you.

Joseph celebrated his eighteenth birthday in May. As we gathered with family and friends, we sang the song, ate the cake, and watched Joseph open presents. One gift was from a young lady Joe was dating at the time. When he opened it, I looked at him with a confused expression. She had given him a watch. It was not just any watch, but a watch just like the one I had given him at Christmas.

I asked, "Did you lose your watch?" He answered, "Sort of." Then he asked, "Dad, do you remember Alex in Panama?" My mind raced back to our trip, and I remembered the moment we met Alex and faced him with no shoebox for a boy his age. Joseph smiled and said, "I gave him my watch."

I had never been more proud of my son than I was at that moment. The watch was a special edition with an emblem of a Ford

Mustang on the side. Joseph was driving a Mustang we bought together. The watch had been a symbol of our father-son connection in that car. But today, the watch was something more. It was a symbol of surrender, sacrifice, and love. It was an emblem of mercy.

Two teenage boys—one Panamanian and the other American—were living a world apart. But they shared an experience that neither of them would ever forget. Joseph's world was one of provision; Alex's world was one of limitation. Joseph recognized that what he had, he had been given. He also knew that what he had been given was his to give in return. And so he did.

In that act of generosity, a connection was made between faith and works, principles and practices, and most important of all, the heart of God and the hearts of men.

a change of heart

> *Worship is giving God the best that He has given you. Be careful what you do with the best you have. Whenever you get a blessing from God, give it back to Him as a love gift. Take time to mediate before God and offer the blessing back to him in a deliberate act of worship.*
>
> —*Oswald Chambers*[2]

The appeal of Romans 12:1–2 is a call to respond to God's mercy from the heart. It is a call to measure all God has done and to let the ocean of God's love and grace flow into the sea of Christian service and living.

The "Panama Canal" of Our Faith

Romans 12:1–2 is the "Panama Canal" of the entire book of Romans. Everything before this passage and everything after this passage in the book of Romans is entirely dependent upon our understanding of the place and purpose of these two verses.

Every reader of Romans is conscious of a distinct break in the train of thought as he moves from 11:36 to 12:1. The theological exposition (or argument) centering around the problem as to how sinful man can be put into right relationship with God is over. But there is more to be said, because when man is made right with his Maker, he needs to know what difference this makes in his relations with his fellowmen. He needs to know what is expected of him and how to apply his new resources to all the situations confronting him.[1]

An Emblem of Mercy

This is the most essential reality in the Bible: we live in faith and response to the God who has loved us, redeemed us, and called us into relationship with Him. All of life becomes a thank-you for God's goodness and grace extended to us.

When I survey the wondrous cross
On which the Prince of glory died,
My richest gain I count but loss,
And pour contempt on all my pride.

Forbid it, Lord, that I should boast,
Save in the death of Christ my God!
All the vain things that charm me most,
I sacrifice them to His blood.

See from His head, His hands, His feet,
Sorrow and love flow mingled down!
Did e'er such love and sorrow meet,
Or thorns compose so rich a crown?

Were the whole realm of nature mine,
That were a present far too small;
Love so amazing, so divine,
Demands my soul, my life, my all.

—Isaac Newton,
"When I Survey the Wondrous Cross"

chapter 7
a change of mind

I have a pair of sunglasses I love to wear. They're more round than oval. When I wear them, I look a bit like John Lennon—without the hair. The frames are bent. The nosepiece on the left side is missing. They are cheap, old, and broken. So why do I still have them, much less wear them?

They are shades of blue. The lenses have a blue tint that makes everything brighter and clearer. The sky, though dimmed by haze, takes on azure radiance and clarity. The grass is not just green; it is spring green. I love the way my shades of blue heighten the quality of everything in my world. (If only my wife and kids could gain appreciation for the way I look when I wear them!)

Perception creates reality. This is a principle we can apply not only to the physical world of sight but to the spiritual world, as well. God's work of grace for us is intended to change the whole of our perception and response to the life we are born to live.

Looking at Life from God's Perspective

When we begin to see our lives through the lens of Scripture, we gain something far greater than "shades of blue." We perceive life in a new and transforming way. We can clearly see that everything we have, we have been given.

Rick Warren's book *The Purpose–Driven Life* begins with these words: "It's not about you."[1] Isn't it amazing that a book that begins with a negative statement, going against the grain in a culture of consumerism, would find such favor and interest? Why? The answer is in the Book—not Rick's book but God's book. "O LORD, I know the way of man is not in himself; it is not in man who walks to direct his own steps" (Jer. 10:23).

We are not self-generated, and we cannot be self-directed. God gives us life, and it is an incredible gift. What we have, we have—by God's grace—been given. And grace changes our total view and perspective of life. The life we have is not our own; we hold it in trust for another. Simply stated, we are His. Therefore, the focus of life is transformed when a new mindset in management takes over.

All that we are and all that we have in life are by God's mercy and grace. Thus the focus of our lives shifts from ownership (what's ours) to stewardship (what's God's). Our job is to be found faithful.

I am convinced many Christians do not understand what it means to be stewards. These believers have been forgiven of their sins and no longer fear the outcome of death; however, they have not understood or embraced the full expression of their salvation by becoming stewards in life. Yet when we begin to see ourselves

> When we begin to see ourselves as God's stewards, everything about us changes from the inside out.

as God's stewards, everything about us changes from the inside out.

Stewardship is the compelling motive and defining perspective of authentic Christian living. Because I am grateful to God for His great mercy toward me and because I desire to honor Him in every part of my life, I want to be a faithful steward. It's a change in how I see life. It's not a shade of blue but the color of mercy on me.

Stewardship living stands in stark contrast and absolute contradiction to the self-indulged, self-absorbed, and self-driven attitudes of the world. Many, if not most, in our world live according to instincts.

By contrast, Christians are driven to give. It is a part of the new nature in Christ and a part of a new focus in stewardship and service. For this reason, Paul calls believers to come apart from the self-focus that is so instinctive of our culture and to become wholly Christlike in our living.

A Call to Spiritual Transformation

Having reminded us of all God has done for us, Paul gives us this challenge: "Do not be conformed to this world, but be transformed by the renewing of your mind, that you may prove what is that good and acceptable and perfect will of God" (Rom. 12:2).

I love the expanded emphasis of the J. B. Phillips translation: "Don't let the world squeeze you into its own mould, but let God re-make you so that your whole attitude of mind is changed. Thus, you will prove in practice that the will of God is good, acceptable to Him, and perfect."

Many live as if they were Play-Doh, constantly shaped and reshaped by the trends of the times. When we are shaped by the world around us and our mindset is consistent with those who live as though there is no God, we are easily squeezed into the world's mold.

> We process all of life differently when we interpret life through the lens of God's mercy.

But Romans 12:2 is a call to a complete change in mindset. We process all of life differently when we interpret life through the lens of God's mercy. His mercy, grace, and love are transformational realities for us. This is the ultimate reality: spirituality that conforms us to the image of Christ. It is God's work to remake and reshape us from the inside out in such a way that we no longer live by self-absorbing and self-preserving instincts; rather, we live to honor and serve the God who made us for Himself.

As we saw in part 1, the Christian life is nothing more and nothing less than new life in Christ. It is a life transformed by God's grace and mercy and now given fully to the purpose of realizing His pleasure and glory in all we do each day.

The most pronounced life shift for a believer is a move from getting all we can out of life to giving our lives away for Jesus Christ. It was Jesus who cut it straight: "Whoever desires to come after Me, let him deny himself, and take up his cross, and follow Me. For whoever desires to save his life will lose it, but whoever loses his life for My sake and the gospel's will save it. For what will it profit a man if he gains the whole world, and loses his own soul?" (Mark 8:34–36).

> God's desire—His very design—is for every believer to bear a greater resemblance to the image of His Son than to the spirit of the age in which we live.

What we have, we have been given. Life is transformed according to God's purpose and plan. This is the opposite of a culture driven toward conformity, acceptance, and adaptation. It is spiritual transformation toward the image of God's Son, Jesus Christ, in us.

The Greek word Paul used for "transformed" in Romans 12:2 means metamorphosis, a complete change from one form to another. It is a metamorphosis when a caterpillar is transformed into a butterfly. The creature no longer crawls; it is renewed through a rebirth, and it soars.

Just as a caterpillar crawls and consumes until it sews itself up in a cocoon, so many people today live for themselves and die alone. But in Christ there is a greater reality. As a butterfly is set free to soar, we, too, are set free in Christ to soar as we serve our Creator. We are intended to live for something higher and greater than merely crawling and consuming. We are made for soaring, serving, and giving.

God works by His Spirit to renew our minds according to a new character and nature. The new nature is like that of Jesus Christ. Paul describes this nature and attitude in Philippians 2: "Let nothing be done through selfish ambition or conceit, but in lowliness of mind let each esteem others better than himself. Let each of you look out not only for his own interests, but also for the interests of others. Let this mind be in you which was also in Christ Jesus, who, being in the form of God, did not consider it robbery to be equal with God, but made Himself of no reputation, taking the form of a bondservant, and coming in the likeness of men" (vv. 3–7).

So God's desire—His very design—is for every believer to bear a greater resemblance to the image of His Son than to the spirit of the age in which we live. The "world," as Paul called it in Romans 12:2, is the sum total of the attitudes, values, opinions, hopes, desires, issues, and concerns of our day. Yet believers are called to a change of mind with regard to all these concerns in order that we may focus on devoting our hearts and minds to God.

A. W. Tozer said, "God salvages the individual by liquidating him and then raising him again to newness of life."[2] Once our perspective changes in the control center of our mind, then the direction of our life changes for the will and glory of God.

Everything we have, we have been given. This truth puts God at the center of every detail in our lives. Every day is a gift that we, in turn, invest for Him.

a change of mind

Don't let the world squeeze you into its own mould, but let God re-make
you so that your whole attitude of mind is changed. Thus, you will prove
in practice that the will of God is good, acceptable to Him, and perfect
(Rom. 12:1–2 PHILLIPS).

Perception creates reality. This is a principle we can apply not only to the physical world of sight but to the spiritual world, as well.

Looking at Life from God's Perspective

When we begin to see our lives through the lens of Scripture, we perceive life in a new and transforming way. We can clearly see that everything we have, we have been given.

> The letter to the Romans is a piece of exuberant and passionate thinking. This is the glorious life of the mind enlisted in the service of God. Paul takes the well-witnessed and devoutly believed fact of the life, death, and resurrection of Jesus of Nazareth and thinks through its implications. . . . What is God up to? What does it mean that Jesus "saves"? What's behind all this, and where is it going?
> —Eugene Peterson

A biblical understanding of life stewardship will transform a person who has made a profession of faith into a fully devoted follower of Jesus Christ. Stewardship is the compelling motive and defining perspective of authentic Christian living.

A Call to Spiritual Transformation

This is the ultimate reality: spirituality that conforms us to the image of Christ.

It is God's work to remake and reshape us from the inside out in such a way that we no longer live by self-absorbing and self-preserving instincts; rather, we live to honor and serve the God who made us for Himself.

"Whoever desires to come after Me, let him deny himself, and take up his cross, and follow Me. For whoever desires to save his life will lose it, but whoever loses his life for My sake and the gospel's will save it. For what will it profit a man if he gains the whole world, and loses his own soul?" (Mark 8:34–36).

As a butterfly is set free to soar, we, too, are set free in Christ to soar as we serve our Creator. We are intended to live for something higher and greater than merely crawling and consuming. We are made for soaring, serving, and giving.

> God salvages the individual by liquidating him and then raising him again to newness of life.
> —A. W. Tozer

chapter 8
a change of will

Everyone gives his or her life for something. What are you giving your life for? Many people simply waste the life they have been given, but some give their lives for things that matter. Have you considered God's will for your life?

In January 1956, five young men and their families were the subjects of a feature article in *Life* magazine. The men ranged in age from twenty-seven to thirty-two, and though they were friends, they resided in different states and represented different organizations in their work.

It was their work that was spotlighted in *Life* magazine. Each of these men had taken their young families and planted themselves in Ecuador. These five men were unknown with regard to notoriety, but they were uncommon in courage and commitment. Their lives all changed in a moment when Roger Youderian, Peter Fleming, Edward McCully, Jim Elliot, and Nick Saint were martyred as they sought to take the gospel of Jesus Christ to the Auca Indians in the jungles of Eastern Ecuador.

Five bright, promising young American men faced a sudden and costly consequence for their faith. But they took the risk joyfully, convinced that it was the will of God for their lives. It is reported that before making the trip into the jungle territory, they sang this hymn:

> We rest on Thee, our Shield and Defender
> Thine is the battle, Thine shall be the praise

When passing through the gates of pearly splendor
Victors, we rest with Thee through endless days.

Five years earlier, Jim Elliot had written in his diary, "When it comes time to die, make sure all you have to do is die." He also wrote in another place, "He is no fool who gives what he cannot keep, to gain what he cannot lose."[1]

Though the earthly lives of these men are over, the end of their story has not yet been written. A tribal leader who took part in the brutal slaying of these five American missionaries later followed Christ. The Auca or Waodani tribes were transformed as the widows of these slain men continued their work in prayer and service and ultimately were successful in taking the gospel to these people. And a generation of missionaries and Christian workers has been inspired, comforted, and challenged by the story first captured in the book *Through Gates of Splendor*, written by Jim Elliot's wife, Elisabeth.

The Reality of God's Will

I remind us of this story because I fear many Christians believe that if they make a complete and radical commitment to do God's will, the ultimate outcome may be death. Of course, for those of you who haven't been reminded lately, we are all going to die eventually. Therefore, the real question is not if you will die; it is how you will live. Will you fully and wholly live for something that really matters?

God's will is not about dying; it is about really living. God wants you and me to live for something that matters. He wants us to live according to His purpose and to spend our lives in pursuit of His holy pleasure.

> God's will is not about dying; it is about really living.

This is the crux of the issue Paul is pressing in Romans 12:2: "Do not conform any longer to the pattern of this world, but be transformed by the renewing of your mind. Then you will be able to test and approve what God's will is—his good, pleasing and perfect will" (NIV).

Far from being a dreaded or fearful pursuit, the will of God is the highest, greatest, and best of all the pathways of life. For this reason, Paul is pleading as if to say, "In light of all God has done for you and in view of all God has called you to do in response to Him, are you willing to live to prove the will of God? And by the way, His will is good, acceptable, and perfect."

> The will of God is the highest, greatest, and best of all the pathways of life.

It's curious that we often think God's will is limiting and potentially distasteful. Where did we ever get that idea? I think that it started with a little conversation with a serpent in a garden. We struggle to believe that God's will is good, acceptable, and perfect. Oh, we might agree that His will is perfect, but *good* and *acceptable*? We have our doubts.

Every generation has an opportunity to prove God's will. And God's will is not as much about dying for Christ as it is about being a living sacrifice for Him. Being a living sacrifice is coming to the place where we can transfer the focus of our life from ourselves to Christ alone.

True faith always calls us to a transfer. It begins when we transfer our trust from our own ability to live a life that pleases God and put our trust in Christ alone for the forgiveness of sins and the gift of eternal life.

But faith is also the operational principle of the Christian life. Faith is a challenge to transfer all we would call our own to Christ. We no longer live for our desires, because a transfer has taken place in our hearts and we want to live out all our days for God's desire.

A Transfer of Wills

If you have surrendered your life to Christ, you know exactly what I am talking about. As you read these words, your heart is racing and your soul is crying out, "Oh God, let me live for You!" You have transferred your will to Christ.

Now when I speak of a "transfer of wills," I'm not speaking about the legal document executed when you die. I heard a story about this once that illustrates my point.

An elderly man progressively lost his hearing. By and large, family and friends would sit and talk—at times ignoring the man's presence in the room. Occasionally he would try to enter the conversation, or others would raise their voices to get his attention.

Frustrated with his lack of hearing, the old man decided to take action and made an appointment to visit an ear, nose, and throat specialist. The physician assessed his need, identified the extent of his problem, and referred him to a local audiologist who kept pace with the latest trends in hearing advances.

Within days, the elderly man was fitted with a state-of-the-art hearing device that proved revolutionary. Surround sound sparked excitement in a world that had grown dull and predominantly silent.

A month passed, and the old man had a follow-up visit with the doctor who assessed him. After some questioning and examination, the doctor said, "It appears you have a near complete restoration."

The old man simply smiled.

The doctor added, "Your family must be thrilled to know you can hear again."

To which the old man replied, "Oh, I haven't told my family yet. I just sit and listen, but I've changed my will three times!"

Unlike the old man in this story, Rick and Elaine have embraced a genuine transfer of wills—they have surrendered their own will and joyfully submitted to the will of Christ for their lives. Rick is a phenomenally successful businessman, and God has blessed them with substantial financial resources. Not long ago, Rick approached me before Christmas and said, "God has been so good to us. Elaine and I don't want to do anything for each other, but together we want to give and help some families in need."

Our church was involved in a number of community outreach efforts, but Rick and Elaine wanted to do something on a personal level. I'm ashamed to admit it, but in my own busyness and distraction during the Christmas season, I failed to follow up with them. Needless to say, I felt terrible when I encountered Rick in the weeks after Christmas.

Rick was gracious. He assured me that my inaction did not stop their generous impulse. But he went on to say, "I want you to know, I really want to help with people you meet who have a need. There will be a future opportunity. And when you hear of it, be sure to give me a call."

As the new year started to roll, weeks turned into months. But then came a second chance.

While making a hospital visit, I received a message to return the call of a woman whose name I did not initially recognize. As we spoke, she said that her daughter and mine were friends. She went on to explain that she was a single parent, and she related her daughter's desperate desire to change schools.

Her daughter was a freshman at a local high school and told her mom that the atmosphere and conditions of her school were making her miserable. She begged her mother to submit an application to attend a Christian school associated with our church. Then the mother leveled with me: "I told her there was no way we could ever afford for her to attend a private school."

After months of resistance, this single mother took a simple step of faith. She filled out an application to the Christian school. She could afford the application fee, so she submitted a request for admission and financial aid. Before long, the response came from the school that her daughter was accepted. The school was able to offer her some financial aid, but the remaining balance was greater than this mother's diligent work and sacrifice could absorb.

Having come so far but still being so far away, she called me to see if I knew of any options. I listened. I sensed the passion and pain in the voice of this mother, who desperately wanted to provide something more for her daughter but didn't know where to turn or how to get it. After she shared, we prayed. I told her that I did not have any ability to tap additional resources but that I would continue to pray.

After we finished talking, I thought about Rick and Elaine. I was uncertain as to whether I should make a call. Private education was not exactly the type of "family need" I understood them to want to provide. However, I decided to let them make the decision and placed the call.

When we spoke later that evening, Rick was planning to leave the country for a business trip to East Asia. Though he was busy getting ready for the trip, he asked me to tell him about the girl and the tuition. And then he said this: "I want you to call this mother back and tell her that we are thrilled to be able to make up the difference for her daughter to make the move to a Christian school this year. And there is something else. We want you to tell her that we will provide the balance of this need until she graduates!" Tears filled my eyes as I heard these words. This was so much more than she or I could have imagined.

Here was a single mother, working hard and sacrificing to do all she could to support and provide for her daughter. She did what she could do, submitted an application, and paid an admission fee. But she could never have imagined how that simple step of faith could be met with God's overwhelming supply.

It wasn't a *money* thing; it was a *will* thing. Rick and Elaine had made a transfer in their hearts, and they were willing to do the will of God. And they wanted to do it in a way that would truly impact the life of another.

A single mother sought God's will for her daughter. A high school student wanted God's will for her future. A couple desired to do God's will with their resources. And as the pastor in the middle, I shared money I didn't have with a mother I didn't know and saw a young woman experience an opportunity I couldn't give and a joy I can't fully describe, all from people pursuing the will of God. His will is good, acceptable, and perfect. No wonder the Psalmist declared,

"Oh, taste and see that the LORD is good; Blessed is the man who trusts in Him!" (Ps. 34:8).

This is not the end of this story; there are still many chapters to be written in the lives I've introduced to you. But I share it to remind us all that when we are willing to give, we discover what it means to really live.

Proving the Will of God

So let's go back to the question at hand: are you willing to "prove" the will of God in your life? Paul says this is what being a "living sacrifice" is all about—proving the will of God.

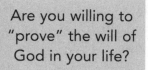

For the past few years, I've consistently read a devotional entitled *Daily with the King* by Glyn Evans. It has been a shelter of comfort and source of encouragement for me. One year as I struggled with God's will in my own life, I opened and started my daily routine, wanting to get through the day's reading and get on to the pressing matters at hand.

In the middle of my reading, God invaded the moment when I read these words:

> I promise to fulfill my function as a "prover of God." That is every Christian's function, regardless of his occupation or spiritual gift. A prover of God brings God out of the Bible and makes Him alive today.
>
> God loves to be proved. "Prove me *now*" (Mal. 3:10 KJV, italics added). "Ask a sign for yourself from the Lord" (Isa. 7:11). He knows that each generation is born skeptical. The Bible must be reborn to every generation. God must break out of print into live action and re-create Bible scenes and activities. Just as God wrote the Bible, so He must repeat the Bible in us.

That is why He needs Abrahams, Gideons, Davids, and Pauls today. In short, He needs God-provers. . . .

Proving God, however, is not easy. It involves the impossible. You do not prove God when you pray for a healing that will occur naturally. Or when you ask God for $10,000 when you already have $20,000 in the bank. Proving God is asking Him to cure the incurable. It is asking Him to give you $10,000 when you have nothing.

But who is sufficient for those heroics? Isn't life fairly humdrum and prosaic? Doesn't God come in the "still small voice" (1 Kings 19:12 KJV)?

If so, there is something wrong with our faith. If Satan is still alive, if sin is still man's habit, and if disease, hunger, and death still stalk, then God must find "provers." He needs the ordinary man who has extraordinary faith.

The question is, am I willing to risk embarrassment and failure to be a prover of God? That is the nub of it all—to dare God and risk everything on His simple Word. Provers of God are always winners with God.

Many fear the demand of sacrifice to be greater than the return of reward. But for those who risk to prove God, His faithfulness exceeds our expectations.

Are you willing to be a "prover of God"?

chapter 8

a change of will

*When we want to be something other than the thing God wants us
to be, we must be wanting what in fact, will not make us happy.*

—*C. S. Lewis*[2]

*Everyone gives his or her life for something. When it
comes time to die, make sure all you have to do is die.*

—*Jim Elliot*

The Reality of God's Will

God's will is not about dying; it is about living. God wants us to live for something that matters. He wants us to live in accordance with His purpose and to spend our lives in pursuit of His holy pleasure.

"Do not conform any longer to the pattern of this world, but be transformed by the renewing of your mind. Then you will be able to test and approve what God's will is—his good, pleasing and perfect will" (Rom. 12:2 NIV).

The apostle Paul is pleading as if to say, "In light of all God has done for you and in view of all God has called you to do in response to Him, are you willing to live to prove the will of God? And by the way, His will is good, acceptable, and perfect."

A Transfer of Wills

God's will is not as much about dying for Christ, but rather being a living sacrifice for Him. Being a "living sacrifice" is coming to the place and persuasion in life to where "me, mine, and ours" is transferred to "Christ and Christ alone."

Proving the Will of God

God wants us to prove Him in our lives day by day.

God loves to be proved. "Prove me now" (Mal. 3:10 KJV, italics added). "Ask a sign for yourself from the Lord" (Isa. 7:11). He knows that each generation is born skeptical. The Bible must be reborn to every generation. God must break out of print into live action and re-create Bible scenes and activities. Just as God wrote the Bible, so He must repeat the Bible in us. That is why He needs Abrahams, Gideons, Davids, and Pauls today. In short, He needs God provers. . . .

The question is, am I willing to risk embarrassment and failure to be a prover of God? That is the nub of it all—to dare God and risk everything on His simple Word. Provers of God are always winners with God.
—*Glyn Evans, Daily with the King*[3]

part 3
a life distributed

Romans 12–16

*Life is a mission. Every other definition of life is false,
and leads all who accept it astray.*

—GUISEPPE MAZZINI

*For whoever desires to save his life will lose it, but
whoever loses his life for My sake will find it.*

—MATTHEW 16:25

chapter 9
we are gifted to serve

Everybody loves a gift. But not all gifts are equally valued or appreciated. Some gifts are surprises; others are not exactly our preference. Some gifts are affectionately known as "white elephants." These are often regifted to others or used for humorous distributions at staff parties and other gatherings. I once had a velvet Elvis that kept coming back to me. It was a large, gaudy roadside painting of the "king of rock and roll." Each year I made an attempt to pass it on at our annual staff Christmas party. I'll never forget the time I came home and found it the next morning—in my shower!

But there are a few gifts that are treasures to be kept for a lifetime. One Christmas, during our seminary days, my dad reached for the lone—and seemingly overlooked—package left under the tree at the end of our family gift exchange. There was no tag, and the small box looked quite innocent. He tossed it across the room to Connie and me and said, "One other little gift."

As we unwrapped the package, we were quite curious. It appeared to be a can of macadamia nuts, which I like but found to be a strange Christmas finale. Then I noticed that Dad and Mom had tears of anticipation in their eyes. "Open it!" they urged. As I did, I noticed a piece of paper tucked inside. It was a travel brochure for Israel. I was scheduled for a May graduation in the coming year, and Mom and Dad had come up with a plan to send Connie and me to the Holy Land as a graduation gift.

We were stunned and delighted. Connie and I were overwhelmed to think we would walk in the footsteps of Jesus as we commenced a lifetime journey of ministry together.

More than a dozen years later, while leading a trip to Israel, I took our group to one of the most desirable of all stops on the tour: the "golden arches" of Jerusalem. At a McDonald's near Ben Yahuda Street, one of our group members noticed the cups picturing Ronald McDonald and the gang. The cups were similar to those in the States, but with one exception: the printing was in Hebrew. Immediately she thought of a little girl she knew. How often had she heard this three-year-old squeal at the sight of the golden arches when she rode with her family past the neighborhood franchise? This would make a great gift!

Back in the States, the woman told the girl she had purchased a special gift for her while in Israel. The three-year-old could hardly wait to see it. On the appointed evening, the woman rode to dinner with the little girl and her mother. The girl was too excited to wait until they reached the restaurant, so she hastily ripped through the paper and ribbons to expose the treasure. The little girl looked at the McDonald's cup . . . then at the floorboard . . . at the cup . . . at the floorboard. Exasperated, she cried, "This isn't a gift!"

The woman couldn't understand the little girl's confusion until she noticed that a similar cup had been discarded on the floorboard earlier that day. Even though the woman thought the three-year-old would enjoy having a Hebrew McDonald's cup from Jerusalem, she immediately realized her mistake. The little girl couldn't read. To her, all writing was just a combination of unintelligible symbols, making both cups look alike. The child couldn't appreciate the uniqueness of the gift.

God's Unique Gifts to Us

Like the little girl, have you missed the uniqueness of the gifts God has given you? Every one of us has been given a unique design, a significant distinctiveness. Before your physical birth, God designed certain genetic codes that are unique to you, such as the color of your hair and eyes, your height, and so on. In addition, at the time you became a believer through faith in Jesus Christ, God uniquely "coded" your spirit with an individualized package of spiritual gifts to equip you for His purpose.

> Every one of us has been given a unique design, a significant distinctiveness.

I am not referring to natural abilities such as being artistic or athletic or having great mental ability. These are indeed gifts that can be used for the glory of God, but they should not be confused with spiritual gifts.

It is also important to distinguish between the *gift* of the Spirit and the *gifts* of the Spirit. The Bible makes it clear that the *gift* of the Spirit is the indwelling presence of Christ living in all people who receive Jesus Christ as their Lord and Savior.

So what are the gifts of the Spirit? They are specific, God-given abilities that enable Christians to serve, glorify, and live for Him. God places believers with specific gifts in distinct areas of service in the church, to enable us to function as one unified and coordinated body under the headship of Jesus Christ. As Paul explains, "God has set the members, each one of them, in the body just as He pleased" (1 Cor. 12:18).

There is a tremendous amount of material in the Bible on the subject of spiritual gifts. Before we look at some of these passages, though, let's cover some basics as we focus on being good stewards of the gifts God has given us.

How Do You See Yourself?

"For I say, through the grace given to me, to everyone who is among you, not to *think* of himself more highly than he ought to *think*, but to *think* . . ." (Rom. 12:3; emphasis added). Do you see it? *Think* . . . *think* . . . *think*. In other words, Paul is saying, "How are you thinking about yourself? How do you see the design of your life?"

> One of the greatest of all spiritual truths we can embrace is this: what God commands us to do, He enables us to do.

If you are a Christian, you are a new person spiritually. The Bible says that "if anyone is in Christ, he is a new creation; old things have passed away; behold, all things have become new" (2 Cor. 5:17). And this new life you have been born to live is the life you are born to give in spiritual service for Christ. God wants us to see our existence through new eyes. He has, in Christ, given us new enablement to live the life He has called and commanded us to live.

One of the greatest of all spiritual truths we can embrace is this: what God commands us to do, He enables us to do.

Three Categories of Spiritual Gifts

According to Scripture, there are types of spiritual gifts given by God. These gifts are mentioned throughout the Bible, but they are highlighted specifically in three passages: Romans 12, 1 Corinthians 12, and Ephesians 4.

For our purposes in this chapter, I will combine these spiritual gifts into three categories: gifts of service, gifts of signs, and gifts of support. Let's take a look.

Gifts of Service

Gifts of service are supernatural enablements for ministry through the church. The apostle Paul lists several of these gifts in Romans 12:

> Having then gifts differing according to the grace that is given
> to us, let us use them: if prophecy, let us prophesy in proportion

to our faith; or ministry, let us use it in our ministering; he who teaches, in teaching; he who exhorts, in exhortation; he who gives, with liberality; he who leads, with diligence; he who shows mercy, with cheerfulness. (vv. 6–8)

Gifts of service in the church include prophecy, ministry, teaching, exhortation, giving, leadership, and mercy. We are to distribute our lives by using the gifts we have been given as a steward of Jesus Christ.

I love the words of Arthur T. Pierson on this subject of spiritual gifts of service:

"Everyone has some gift, therefore all should be encouraged. No one has all the gifts, therefore all should be humble. All gifts are for the one Body, therefore all should be harmonious. All gifts are from the Lord, therefore all should be contented. All gifts are mutually helpful and needful, therefore all should be studiously faithful. All gifts promote the health and strength of the whole Body, therefore none can be safely dispensed with. All gifts depend on His fullness for power, therefore all should keep in close touch with Him."[1]

Gifts of Signs

I believe the Bible distinguishes between gifts of *service* and *signs*. In 1 Corinthians 12, the apostle Paul describes some gifts of *service*, but he also mentions specific gifts of signs.

There are diversities of gifts, but the same Spirit. There are differences of ministries, but the same Lord. And there are diversities of activities, but it is the same God who works all in all. But the manifestation of the Spirit is given to each one for the profit of all: . . . to another gifts of healings by the same Spirit, to another the working of miracles, to another prophecy, to another discerning of spirits, to another different kinds of tongues,

to another the interpretation of tongues. But one and the same
Spirit works all these things, distributing to each one individu-
ally as He wills. (vv. 4–7, 9–11)

The gifts of signs—tongues, miracles, healings—were given to provide authenticity to the messengers of the church, specifically to the
apostles and the early church. As we read about the first-century
church, we see a tremendous explosion of signs and wonders and miracles. However, in the New Testament, the gifts of signs were not given
to every believer in every place.
They were given specifically to the
places where the apostles and the
disciples established the work of
the church. God used the gifts of
signs to establish the church.

> We are to distribute
> our lives by using the
> gifts we have been
> given as a steward
> of Jesus Christ.

The nature and expression of
sign gifts has been the source of
some controversy in recent years. It is beyond the scope and intent of
this book to address all aspects of this controversy. However, I will
point out that it has always been of interest to me that the majority of
Paul's discussion of issues surrounding the sign gifts occurs in 1
Corinthians, a letter that is aimed at correcting confusion and refo-
cusing service in the church.

This is an important lesson for all of us: distractions will always
delay and diminish our distribution of the gifts God designed for us
to use for His glory.

Gifts of Support

The Bible defines another category of gifts that are unique and
distinct within the ministry of the local church—the gifts of *support*.

And He Himself gave some to be apostles, some prophets, some
evangelists, and some pastors and teachers, for the equipping of

the saints for the work of ministry, for the edifying of the body of Christ, till we all come to the unity of the faith and of the knowledge of the Son of God, to a perfect man, to the measure of the stature of the fullness of Christ; that we should no longer be children, tossed to and fro and carried about with every wind of doctrine, by the trickery of men, in the cunning craftiness of deceitful plotting, but, speaking the truth in love, may grow up in all things into Him who is the head—Christ—from whom the whole body, joined and knit together by what every joint supplies, according to the effective working by which every part does its share, causes growth of the body for the edifying of itself in love. (Eph. 4:11–16)

These gifts of support—including apostleship, prophecy, evangelism, and teaching—were given to the apostles and prophets who laid the foundation of the church. Today, gifts of support are given to encourage every believer to grow and mature in the body of Christ. The Bible says that God gives these gifts to church evangelists, pastors, and teachers for the building up of the body of Christ until every member comes to the maturity of faith.

Characteristics of Spiritual Gifts

Enablement. Establishment. Encouragement. This is how the Bible presents the subject of spiritual gifts. But in every case, spiritual gifts share certain key characteristics. Let's examine four of these characteristics in detail.

Supernatural in Origin

Sometimes I think we have the idea that only the sign gifts are supernatural. Other times, I think we put all of our focus on discovering our spiritual gifts and pay little attention to actually using our gifts. Yet wherever Christians are working and fulfilling the activity of God in their lives, they exhibit the supernatural power of God through the Holy Spirit.

Whenever a spiritual gift is in operation—even if it is someone with the gift of service changing a dirty diaper in a church nursery—it is as much the power of God as someone who speaks in tongues.

Personal in Distribution

The Bible makes it clear that every Christian receives an individualized spiritual gift: "As God has dealt to *each one*" (Rom. 12:3; emphasis added).

I like to think of spiritual gifts as primary colors on the Master's color pallet, and God mixes, blends, and applies those gifts in the church according to the purposes He wants to achieve through my life and yours.

Functional in Design

Spiritual gifts are not delicate, shiny objects to be placed behind a glass case on display in the church. They are not to be admired or debated; they are to be *used*. Spiritual gifts are like tools in a toolbox. Every one is sturdy and solid and usable for the building up of the body of Christ.

First Corinthians 12:4–7 makes it clear that God intends us to use our spiritual gifts for the good of all believers: "There are diversities of gifts, but the same Spirit. There are differences of ministries, but the same Lord. And there are diversities of activities, but it is the same God who works all in all. But the manifestation of the Spirit is given to each one for the profit of all." It's tragic to see believers who fail to deploy their God-given gifts through the local church.

Beneficial to Others

God has given us spiritual gifts so that we might benefit other members of the body of Christ and the mission of that body in the world. Just as your human body benefits from all the members functioning together, so the spiritual body of Christ benefits when all its members are functioning together.

It is amazing how our physical body is affected by an injured or disabled part of the body. For example, if you constantly favor an injured arm, over time you may start having pain in your shoulder, back, or neck. Every member needs to be healthy and working for the benefit of the whole body! When one member of that body is not working, the rest of the body carries the weight of the dysfunctional member.

God intends us to use our spiritual gifts for the good of all believers.

The life we are born to live in Christ is the life we are born to give for Christ. It is a life distributed. And this distribution begins with the church—the body of Christ. Our shared life in Christ through our spiritual gifts is where we begin the adventure of living beyond ourselves.

chapter 9
we are gifted to serve

God uniquely "coded" your spirit with an individualized package of spiritual gifts to equip you for His purpose.

God's Unique Gifts to Us

Your spiritual gift is a stewardship—a life tool—you have been given by God to maximize your life mission and service for His glory.

"For I say, through the grace given to me, to everyone who is among you, not to think *of* himself more highly than he ought to think, but to *think . . .*" (Rom. 12:3; emphasis added).

What Are Spiritual Gifts?

Everyone has some gift, therefore all should be encouraged. No one has all the gifts, therefore all should be humble. All gifts are for the one Body, therefore all should be harmonious. All gifts are from the Lord, therefore all should be contented. All gifts are mutually helpful and needful, therefore all should be studiously faithful. All gifts promote the health and strength of the whole Body, therefore none can be safely dispensed with. All gifts depend on His fullness for power, therefore all should keep in close touch with Him.
—Arthur T. Pierson

Three Categories of Spiritual Gifts

Gifts of *service* are supernatural enablements for ministry through the church.

Gifts of *signs* were given to provide authenticity to the messengers of the church, specifically to the apostles and the early church. God used signs to establish the church.

Gifts of *support* were given to the church apostles and prophets who laid the foundation of the church. Gifts of support are also given today for the encouragement of every believer to grow and mature in the body of Christ.

Enablement. Establishment. Encouragement. This is how the Bible presents the subject of spiritual gifts. But in every case, spiritual gifts are supernatural and they involve faithful stewardship.

Characteristics of Spiritual Gifts

Spiritual gifts are . . .
• supernatural in origin
• personal in distribution
• functional in design
• beneficial for service

chapter 10
we are lifted to love

On a cold January morning, thirteen men made a routine descent into the Sago coal mine in West Virginia. The chain of events that set off an explosion in that mine is not altogether clear. For forty-two hours, the men were trapped beneath the surface. When their families heard the news, they gathered together, desperately praying that the rescue efforts would be successful.

The headline in the first-edition copies of *USA Today* proclaimed ALL ALIVE, but by the time most people got to the newsstands, the worst of all fears was realized. Twelve men would never again see the faces of their loved ones. All the men perished. All but one, that is—Randy McCloy.

Randy suffered severe carbon monoxide poisoning and was at the doorway of death when someone finally reached him. His rescue was the one glimmer of light in the dark shadows of this collapsed mine.

He spent weeks in a coma and months in a rehabilitation hospital. Gradually, his limited responses returned. The most telling was the day his wife, Anna, stood at his bedside. She knew he could not talk, so she said, "Randy, if you know who I am, give me a kiss." To her shock and joy, Randy responded to her request. He leaned up and kissed her.

His first definitive response was a gesture of love.

As I reflected on this story, I was reminded of the incredible power of love. For all of the damage done to Randy's lungs, nothing could stop the power of love from beating in his heart. In many ways, it was love that delivered him from death's doorway to a hospital room and then to his home for a reunion with the family he so deeply loved.

Gradually, Randy began to talk about the hours he spent beneath the surface with his fellow workers. He was reluctant to discuss the details of the final moments of his friends and coworkers, but he did speak of the actions of these men as death approached. In particular, Randy said, all of the men wrote farewell notes to their loved ones. He said, "It's a hard thing to have to say good-bye to someone on a piece of paper." Randy himself had written a note in which he declared his love and affection for Anna, told his son and namesake Randall to "trust in the Lord," and encouraged his daughter Isabelle to "stay sweet." In this love letter, he told his family that he did not want them to grieve long but to be happy and live.[1]

As these men took their final breaths in the darkness, they painstakingly scrawled out love letters to the ones they would leave behind. How great is the power of love!

The Bible is God's love letter written to a lost world. It is a letter of comfort, strength, and hope written to all who believe. It is a book about relationships. From cover to cover, the Bible describes our relationship to God through Jesus Christ and the relationship we have with others.

In the New Testament, the Greek word translated "fellowship" is *koinonia*, which means to have in common, to share. It means having the same life. As brothers and sisters in God's family, we have a common life in Jesus Christ.

Our family relationship with other believers also means that we share the same love. We have the transforming power of the love of God inside. Once we are right with God through His Son, Jesus Christ, then everyone who comes in contact with us experiences something new and different.

In my opinion, nothing makes a church more attractive than love. When love is in the house—the church house, that is—there is a spirit of warmth, service, and sacrifice that draws other people to the family of God. When genuine biblical love is absent, a church becomes selfish and snobbish.

In Romans 12, having discussed God's gracious provision of gifts for Christian service, Paul begins to write about love. These key ideas and messages from the heart are to be embraced and shared.

Affirm the Principle of Love

Love one another! This is the foundational principle of the Christian life.

The Bible tells us that God is love (1 John 4:8). All true love has its source and culmination in God Himself. And this love can only be realized through Jesus Christ, the Mediator of God's love for us. That is why having a relationship with God through Christ is so critical. We will always be empty of true love until we have experienced the love of God. That uplink, that sense of getting connected and getting into God's network, is a critical part of living the life God wants us to give.

In Matthew 22, a group of people came to Jesus and tried to trap Him in a debate over the law. They asked, "What is the most important law?" Jesus replied, "You shall love the LORD your God with all your heart, with all your soul, with all your mind, and with all your strength. This is the first commandment" (Mark 12:30). Jesus said all of the Law is summed up in this: loving God and loving others. The authenticating mark of true Christian living is the presence of God's love in our lives.

> Love one another! This is the foundational principle of the Christian life.

Shortly before His death and resurrection, Jesus reminded His disciples of the importance of loving one another. He said, "A new commandment I give to you, that you love one another; as I have loved you, that you also love one another. By this all will know that you are My disciples, if you have love for one another" (John 13:34–35).

Love is the authenticating mark of true biblical Christianity. It is the seal and emblem upon the heart of every person who belongs to Jesus Christ.

Apply the Practice of Love

How are Christians to take God's love and transfer it into the fellowship of the church of Jesus Christ? How is that love to be seen, and what is that love to motivate us to do? How are we to constantly stir up the love of Christ in our lives when we come together as the people of God?

As Paul continues his discussion about love, he writes in short, simple sentences to be embraced and remembered: "Let love be without hypocrisy. Abhor what is evil. Cling to what is good. Be kindly affectionate to one another with brotherly love, in honor giving preference to one another; not lagging in diligence, fervent in spirit, serving the Lord; rejoicing in hope, patient in tribulation, continuing steadfastly in prayer; distributing to the needs of the saints, given to hospitality" (Rom. 12:9–13).

> Love is the authenticating mark of true biblical Christianity.

Paul is passionate and direct as he provides specific guidance, like bullet points in a list, of how to apply this principle of love in our lives. I like to call these the Ten Commandments of Christian Fellowship.

1. Create an Atmosphere of Authenticity

"Let love be without hypocrisy" (Rom. 12:9).

If I could paraphrase what Paul is saying in this verse, it is simply this: create an atmosphere of authenticity, because there is no greater vice in the church than hypocrisy. Hypocrisy destroys the integrity of a church and stands in contradiction to the very character of what Christians are to be. As representatives of Christ in this world, Christians are to be true at demonstrating love, and hypocrisy is nothing more than role-play and acting.

When Jesus was praying in the Garden of Gethsemane with His disciples, a band of soldiers came from the city of Jerusalem. Leading the soldiers was one of Jesus's twelve closest followers: Judas Iscariot. Judas came forward and greeted Jesus with a kiss. At that signal, the soldiers and others who were there seized Jesus and took Him through an unlawful trial. I find it interesting that the Gospel of Luke records Jesus asking Judas, "How can you betray me, the Son of Man, with a kiss?" (Luke 22:48 NLT).

I wonder how many of us betray the Lord Jesus Christ with actions that seem to be a kiss of love for His people, for His church, and for His work, but our motives reveal a betrayal of hypocrisy. Hypocrisy is betrayal with a kiss! Paul warns us not to be pretenders.

Judson Swihart writes of the tragedy of those who do not experience the freedom of genuine love: "Some people are like medieval castles. Their high walls keep them safe from being hurt. They protect themselves emotionally by permitting no exchange of feelings with others. No one can enter. They are secure from attack. However, inspection of the occupant finds him or her lonely, rattling around the castle alone. The castle-dweller is a self-made prisoner. He or she needs to feel loved by someone, but the walls are so high that it is difficult to reach out or for anyone else to reach in."[2]

Jesus, who told us that we were to love one another in John 13:34–35, preceded His instruction that night by laying aside his outer garments, taking a towel and a basin of water, and kneeling to wash the feet of His disciples. Talk about a love that is vulnerable and authentic! The Savior willingly took upon Himself the form of a servant. And if we are going to show the reality of Christ's love in us, we have to begin by creating a spirit of authenticity in the church.

2. Guard Against the Injury of Impurity

The Bible says, "Abhor what is evil. Cling to what is good" (Rom. 12:9). While it is true that the church is to be an authentic place where everyone is valued and accepted, not all behavior is acceptable. To truly love someone is to hate what destroys that person.

"[Love] does not rejoice in iniquity, but rejoices in the truth" (1 Cor. 13:6). If you love someone, you cannot stand by silently while you watch the antithesis of love destroy your loved one. There is something about your love for the other person that makes you want to fight for what is right for your loved one.

Love seeks the highest good and best for another. Even though God is love, He is not permissive. You can't say you love God if you are living below the standards God established to protect us in love. Covetousness, greed, lying, homosexuality, adultery, every form of moral impurity, pride, lust, hatred—the Bible says if you are indulging and engaging in these things, you are the antithesis of love! God abhors what is evil, so cling to what is good.

> **Even though God is love, He is not permissive.**

3. Express Affection Openly

"Be kindly affectionate to one another with brotherly love" (Rom. 12:10).

The Greek phrase used in this verse is *philos storge*, "family love." What do family members do when they come together? They embrace, hug, kiss, and greet one another. Like Randal McCloy, they find a way to express their depth of affection. The church of Jesus Christ should be a place where the atmosphere is like a family reunion. We ought to express affection openly to one another, because the love of God is expressed love.

On a few occasions, just for fun, I have asked people in gatherings where I am speaking how many believe that we should obey the Bible. On every occasion, hands are raised all over the room. Then I ask them to look at the person sitting next to them as I read Romans 16:16: "Greet one another with a holy kiss." You can imagine the laughter that breaks out. I quickly backtrack just to be sure no one takes advantage of the situation!

What does Paul mean when he tells Christians to "greet one another with a holy kiss"? In the ancient world, as well as today in the Middle East, both men and women greet one another by kissing on both sides of the face, on each cheek. That is a common greeting in that culture. Most Westerners do not greet one another that way today, except for those with whom we are intimate. Instead, we greet one another with a handshake. Regardless of specific cultural practices, Christians are to constantly show brotherly love and affection to one another with a handshake, a hug, words of affirmation and kindness, and expressions of love to one another.

> The love of God is expressed love.

Authentic Christian love reaches and releases. I cannot think of any greater expression of love than a nail-pierced hand stretched out to us. And that same One who stretched out His nail-pierced hand to us has commanded us to stretch out our hands to one another.

4. Develop an "Others" Mentality

" . . . in honor giving preference to one another" (Rom. 12:10).

Fellowship and selfishness cannot coexist. They are mutually exclusive. If you walk through the door of the church thinking, *What can others do for me here?* you have destroyed the bonds of fellowship in that church. But when there is authentic affection for one another, then we seek to serve and give preference to others in fellowship.

Popular Scottish theologian William Barclay writes, "More than half the trouble that arises in churches concerns rights and privileges and prestige. Someone has not been given his or her place, someone has been neglected or unthanked. The mark of a truly Christian man has always been humility."[3]

Humility is not thinking lowly of yourself; it is having the strength to focus on others instead of yourself.

5. *Maintain a Spirit of Urgency*

". . . not lagging in diligence, fervent in spirit, serving the Lord" (Rom. 12:11).

As a church, we cannot lose our zeal. Our worship services should be filled with celebration, not stagnation. We celebrate a risen and living Savior! But sadly, the battle cry for far too many Christians is, "I couldn't care less."

Lest you think all I am talking about is emotion and hype, let's look again at how the apostle Paul describes this kind of zeal: "not lagging in diligence, fervent in spirit, serving the Lord" (Rom. 12:11). The outlet of our fervency for Christ is to be the spirit of service to the Lord, taking the opportunity to serve and honor the Lord. This is the practical expression of love toward those around us.

6. *Live Positively*

" . . . rejoicing in hope . . ." (Rom. 12:12).

A church cannot have positive fellowship with negative people. God is the One who gives us hope. While we go through hard times, we live positively because we have hope in Jesus Christ!

7. *Cultivate Endurance and Tenacity*

" . . . patient in tribulation . . . " (Rom. 12:12).

We need to help one another be strong in the hardships of life. When it comes to the trials and hardships, we are to be spiritual bulldogs—determined to persevere and prevail.

One of the keys to strong fellowship is bearing the responsibility of going through the hardships of life. We should exercise a bulldog determination that will be patient in tribulation and cultivate endurance and tenacity in our lives. During times of suffering, we look to Jesus, "consider Him who endured such hostility from sinners against Himself" lest we become "weary and discouraged" (Heb. 12:3).

8. Continue Together in Prayer

". . . continuing steadfastly in prayer . . ." (Rom. 12:12).

Many of us would have put prayer at the top of the list of commands for Christian fellowship. However, the apostle Paul just put it in the cycle. He said that prayer should be a part of everything we do. As believers in the body of Christ, we should be constantly continuing in prayer, because true intimacy is built

> Prayer is the means by which God supplies grace for every trial and gives strength for every temptation.

when the church learns to pray for one another and to pray together. Prayer is the means by which God supplies grace for every trial and gives strength for every temptation.

9. Have a Heart of Generosity

". . . distributing to the needs of the saints . . ." (Rom. 12:13).

In a world that is bent on *getting*, Christians are bent on *giving*. That is why we constantly make much of this issue of giving, because nothing plays more to the core of who we are and our values than what we do with our possessions. Let love be expressed in a tangible way through giving. Whom do you know in need?

10. Give Yourselves to Hospitality

". . . given to hospitality . . ." (Rom. 12:13)

What a practical instruction! When the fellowship of the church is real, the church has a spirit of hospitality and is open to receiving others.

It is interesting to note the close association of the words *hospitality* and *hospital*. A hospital is a place where people are taken just like they are. Likewise, churches should reflect a spirit of openness and acceptance. Jesus said, "Those who are well have no need of a physician, but those who are sick" (Luke 5:31).

That brings us back to the hospital—the place where Randy McCloy was surrounded by the warmth of loving hearts after being rescued from the darkness of the Sago coal mine. Randy has started a new life. And while he is the sole survivor of one of the worst mining accidents in American history, his life is a clear reminder of the power of love.

A man wisely observed, "The churches would soon be filled if outsiders could find that people in the churches loved them when they came in. . . . We must win them to us first, then we can win them to Christ. We must get the people to love us, and then turn them over to Christ." Before you think these words a statement of a modern-day religious marketeer, let me say that those are the words of the evangelist Dwight L. Moody, spoken more than one hundred years ago.

> Get people to love you, and then people will love Jesus.

Get people to love you, and then people will love Jesus. If people are welcome in your church, they are more likely to welcome your Savior.

While it's been a long time since I have sung this old melody, the message still speaks to my heart:

> I was sinking deep in sin, far from the peaceful shore,
> Very deeply stained within, sinking to rise no more;
> But the Master of the sea heard my despairing cry,
> From the waters lifted me, now safe am I.
> Love lifted me! Love lifted me!
> When nothing else could help, love lifted me.
> Love lifted me! Love lifted me!
> When nothing else could help, love lifted me![4]

chapter 10
we are lifted to love

You have not lived today until you have done something
for someone who cannot pay you back.

—*John Bunyan*

Affirm the Principle of Love

Love one another! This is the foundational principle of the Christian life.

Apply the Practice of Love

Put into daily practice the Ten Commandments of Christian Fellowship:

1. Create an atmosphere of authenticity. "Let love be without hypocrisy" (Rom. 12:9).

2. Guard against the injury of impurity. "Abhor what is evil. Cling to what is good" (Rom. 12:9).

Even though God is love, He is not permissive. Some find it difficult to distinguish between weakness and forgiveness.

3. Express affection openly. "Be kindly affectionate to one another with brotherly love" (Rom. 12:10).

4. Develop an "others" mentality. "In honor giving preference to one another" (Rom. 12:10).

More than half the trouble that arises in churches concerns rights and privileges and prestige. Someone has not been given his or her place, someone has been neglected or unthanked. The mark of a truly Christian man has always been humility.
—William Barclay

5. Maintain a spirit of urgency. ". . . not lagging in diligence, fervent in spirit, serving the Lord" (Rom. 12:11).

6. Live positively. ". . . rejoicing in hope . . ." (Rom. 12:12).

A church cannot have positive fellowship with negative people. God is the One who gives us hope.

7. Cultivate endurance and tenacity. ". . . patient in tribulation . . ." (Rom. 12:12).

We need to help each other to be strong in the hardships of life.

8. Continue together in prayer. ". . . continuing steadfastly in prayer . . ." (Rom. 12:12).

Prayer is the means by which God supplies grace for every trial and gives strength for every temptation.

9. Have a heart of generosity. ". . . distributing to the needs of the saints . . ." (Rom. 12:13).

In a world that is bent on getting, the Christian is bent on giving.

10. Give yourselves to hospitality. ". . . given to hospitality . . ." (Rom. 12:13).

It is interesting to note the close association of the words *hospitality* and *hospital*. A hospital is a place where people are taken just like they are. Likewise, the church is to be the starting point where people come and receive a spirit of openness and acceptance. Jesus said that those who are well do not need a physician, but those who are sick.

Love lifted me!

chapter 11
we are shaped by experiences

Life is a series of experiences, a chain of daily events that stretch us, try us, grow us, and overwhelm us. Life's experiences can be positive, good, and enjoyable—or they can be painful, frustrating, and difficult.

Recently, I was on a predawn flight from Virginia to Texas. What would have been an otherwise routine flight had one interruption: we stopped in Atlanta. In fact, we ended up sitting on the runway for three hours. Needless to say, my fellow passengers and I were not happy campers.

Yet for all of the hassles and headaches of such an experience, I was impressed by the good humor and professional attention of the flight attendants. What brought frustration and interruption to our travel plans was suddenly adjusted in perspective when the flight attendants requested our support to say thank you to a group of military personnel onboard. We learned that these brave men and women were embarking on a tour of duty in Iraq. Suddenly, our three-hour wait and the hassle of an amended schedule did not seem as important. The attitude of the passengers changed as we considered the greater challenge of the difficulties and demands that this group of enlisted soldiers was facing. In fact, I realized that spending three extra hours on American soil was anything but a hassle to these men and women.

Blessed Are the Flexible

Many, if not most, of life's experiences are beyond our control. They are simply events to which we must respond and adjust. And because life is full of surprises, adjusting is essential. As my good friend Andrew Barbar often reminds me, "Blessed are the flexible, for they rarely get bent out of shape."

As we go through life, we are shaped by our family experiences, educational experiences, spiritual experiences, vocational experiences, ministry experiences, and painful or sorrowful experiences.

God uses all of these experiences of life to test us, to mature us, and to provide ministry to others through us. In fact, some of our greatest opportunities for ministry often come through some of our most painful experiences. The very things that we are prone to resent and regret can become, by God's grace, platforms of grace, mercy, and help in the life of others.

> We are to be good stewards of all our life experiences, both good and bad.

When we embrace the truth that the life we are born to live is the life we are born to give, even hardships have a place in the work and plan of God in our lives. We are to be good stewards of all our life experiences, both good and bad. God never wastes anything in our lives.

Given the fact that some of the things that happen to us are neither enjoyable nor even acceptable, how are we to respond? Listen to what the apostle Paul has to say on this subject:

> Repay no one evil for evil. Have regard for good things in the sight of all men. If it is possible, as much as depends on you, live peaceably with all men. Beloved, do not avenge yourselves, but rather give place to wrath; for it is written, "Vengeance is Mine, I will repay," says the Lord. Therefore "If your enemy is hungry, feed him; if he is thirsty, give him a drink; for in so doing you will heap coals of fire on his head." Do not be overcome by evil, but overcome evil with good. (Rom. 12:17–21)

God tells us that rather than responding to difficult situations with resistance, revenge, and a demand for immediate restitution, there is another way. In the injuries of life, we become a "living sacrifice" (Rom. 12:1).

This call to give our lives as a sacrifice is neither a passive dismissal of our pain nor a denial of our struggle; instead, it is a decisive action based on absolute assurance that while we have surrendered our rights, God will not overlook our concerns. Instead, He tells us that His good, acceptable, and perfect will is to overcome the evils of life with good. This is only possible if you have dealt with the all-encompassing concept of total surrender to Christ.

Life Hurts

Romans 12:17 begins with a simple admission of the facts: Life hurts. Evil is a reality in life. You will not escape the injury of evil in this world.

The most likely and natural of all human responses to the injury of evil is to settle the score and get revenge. Many walk around every day with IOUs in their mental pockets, constantly bringing to mind the people who have done them wrong and thinking of ways they can "make it right." Their motto is, "Don't just get even; get revenge."

> Anger happens, but it cannot go unchecked and unnoticed.

One of the things I am learning is that when I am hurt, injured, or offended, it's impossible for me to be neutral. Anger is a real and common emotion. Anger is our instinctive response to injury. Just think of your finger when pinched or smashed. Your response is not neutral; it is intense. It is hot with anger. If you are not careful, you may say something in the anger of the moment that you may later regret.

Anger is natural and normal, but it can be a dangerous, deadly, and defiling emotion. When not handled appropriately, it is an acid that will destroy any container that harbors it.

Warning light! Anger happens, but it cannot go unchecked and unnoticed. The apostle Paul urges us, "Be angry, and do not sin: do not let the sun go down on your wrath, nor give place to the devil" (Eph. 4:26–27).

Thus we are given in Romans 12:17–21 a guide for "disarmament" in life. In this passage, the apostle Paul gives us sound principles to embrace in the hard and painful experiences of life.

Challenge the Principle of Payback

Our world is filled with people who have at one time or another experienced unjust treatment and undeserved injury. No one—*no one!*—gets through life unharmed. It may not be at the same place, time, or season in life, but we all face injury.

I don't want to downplay the impact of injury in life: death, divorce, accidents, illness, theft, rape, molestation, murder, alcohol, drugs . . . this list could go on for pages. And when we go through these painful experiences, our first thought often turns to the principle of payback.

Doesn't the Bible teach, "an eye for an eye, a tooth for a tooth" (Deut. 19:21 NCV)? Yes. But this principle was given to provide a structure or guide for law. This Old Testament concept established a standard of measure and a statute of limitations for civil offenses.

Civil justice is important, and God provided government to address and deal with social justice. We will learn more about this

> When we try to repay evil with evil, we ourselves get defiled.

in our study of Romans 13 in the next chapter. Yet in these final verses of Romans 12, we are provided guidance to deal with our individual responses to the injuries of life. Great misunderstanding occurs when we try to become judge and jury in our own judicial system of life. The results are never positive when we take the law into our own hands.

The problem with payback is that it is hard to establish sufficient installments that bring balance to the debt incurred. When we try to repay evil with evil, we ourselves get defiled.

For this reason, Booker T. Washington once wrote, "I will not allow any man to make me lower myself by hating him."

Concentrate on Doing Good and Keeping Peace

Doing good and keeping peace are to be at all times and in all ways our life focus. This is the spiritual secret for maintaining balance and well-being in life even when things are against us.

While I can't control what others do to me or escape the inevitable injuries of living in a fallen world, I can choose how I will respond and what happens in my spirit.

I'm the first to admit, this is hard to do. We all want to get even. We want to go after others who have injured us and those we love. We want to make things right when we feel wronged. This is why possibly the hardest teaching of Jesus is found in Matthew 5:38–48, when He challenges us to turn the other cheek when we are offended by someone.

Ruth Graham reports an occasion when she found her daughter Anne slapping her son Franklin back and forth on the face. When Ruth asked her daughter what she was doing, Anne replied, "Mommy, I'm teaching him to turn the other cheek."

The apostle Paul's instruction on our relationships with others continues in Romans 12:17: "Have regard for good things in the sight of all men." In other words, let your attitude and response be right even when you are wronged. And that includes how you respond and deal with those you feel owe you something more in

> Let your attitude and response be right even when you are wronged.

life. Therefore, our perspective is not one of getting even; instead, we are to focus our attention on getting ahead. The way to get ahead is to move beyond the agenda of the vendetta and to stay above the fray of revenge.

We get ahead by following this instruction: "If it is possible, as much as depends on you, live peaceably with all men" (Rom. 12:18). As believers, our goal is to be peacemakers, not troublemakers.

But note this: the call to be a peacemaker in this verse is preceded by a conditional qualification: "If it is possible." Here, Paul is asking us to make sure that it is never said that we are the initiators and instigators of trouble with others.

You can't make peace with everyone; some people have wars in their hearts. You can't right every wrong. You can't remove the consequence of every action. You can't get along with everyone. Understand this undeniable fact of life, and deal with it.

Now, some think that "keeping peace" means going easy on everyone. No, no! Sometimes it takes a standard of strength and right to keep wrong from prevailing. For example, let's say that a husband leaves his wife and children for another woman. She can attempt forgiveness and reconciliation, but if he chooses to refuse and rebel, he can and should experience the consequences of loss and responsibility for his actions.

> If you surrender the matter to God, He promises to settle it for you.

Keeping peace does not necessarily mean "going easy" on someone who has offended us. Instead, it is taking the responsibility to redeem, restore, and make things right with that person.

Our job is to do our best, for the best, and to guard our spirit throughout the process.

Comfort Your Heart with God's Promise

"'Vengeance is Mine, I will repay,' says the Lord" (Rom. 12:19). May I remind you that this is the Word of God! God promises revenge. It is a character issue for Him.

"I will repay." In God's divine time, in His perfect wisdom, and according to His unfailing righteousness, God has backed this promise.

The wrath of God will come. If you try to "settle the score" with someone who has offended you, then you close God out. However, if you surrender the matter to God, He promises to settle it for you.

Injuries become issues of faith. This is why it becomes a stewardship. It is the stewardship of trusting God and the stewardship of letting God work in and through you.

Choose the Stewardship of Good over Evil

When injury comes and we experience setbacks in life, we are not to sit back and wait; we are to go forward and walk with God. What are we to do? Work for good.

Here we are called to demonstrate the ultimate expression of a "transformed mind"—that of moving beyond our impulse for retaliation to the renewal of all of life being lived for God's purpose and glory.

We are challenged to become stewards of our hardships, injuries, and offenses so that we are able to use these experiences to help us live lives of goodness that bring glory to God.

Every year, my family receives a Christmas card from the Barrett family. I had the joy of officiating Mike and Susan's wedding in 1991. They were married in a beautiful and elegant ceremony in a mansion called Thistle Hill in Fort Worth, Texas.

Today, the Barretts are a family of six. It's been a wonderful privilege to observe the expansion and maturity of this family through the years. On their fifth anniversary, Mike and Susan traveled to Florida, where we lived at the time, and were at our church on the Sunday my daughter, Lizzi, made public her commitment to Christ.

Mike is a successful businessman in the technology sector. He has a passion for students and is involved in a ministry targeting juvenile detention centers, seeking to help young people make future choices that will change their life direction. When I look at Mike and Susan, I see a vibrant marriage, solid parents, and a family engaged in many good works. But it could have been different.

When Mike was nine years old, he faced an unthinkable tragedy. Mike's dad was a Kentucky state trooper. Six days before Christmas in 1971, Mike's dad returned home after working the night shift in much need of a few hours of sleep. As he got out of his car, someone appeared from behind the steps at his home. Without explanation or warning, the attacker unloaded several rounds into Mike's dad, killing him instantly. This brutal murder happened right outside young Michael's window.

Needless to say, Mike's world was turned upside down. At the young age of twenty-seven, his mother suddenly found herself a widow with two boys to raise. Mike's life was one of hardship; his family struggled emotionally and financially. Mike related to me the difficulty of growing up without a dad. He had no one to attend his Little League ballgames or fish with him. Throughout his childhood and teenage years, he longed for a mentor, a hero, and a friend.

To this day, no suspect has been apprehended for the murder of Mike's father. It's just an unexplained and undeserved tragedy that marked the life of a nine-year-old boy, his brother, and their young mother. Mike knows it is unlikely he will ever know who killed his father or why this tragedy occurred.

Mike has many reasons to feel cheated in life. But nothing could be further from his attitude and outlook. He is a wonderful husband, an incredible dad, and one of the finest Christian men I know. His service and involvement with troubled young people is even more amazing in light of the tragedy he faced as a child. In fact, on his first youth prison mission trip, he was able, through God's grace, to share the love of Christ with a student who had shot a police officer.

So what is Mike's secret for dealing with such difficulty? He told me, "I may never know who killed my dad, but that is ultimately God's judgment and not mine. Whether the murder case is solved this side of heaven, God only knows and He will make what is wrong here, right there." And then Mike said something that took me aback: "God tells us to live abundantly. I've simply chosen through the years to live above all of this. I will not let it guide my life, but I will live abundantly for Christ."

You know what? The Mike I know does just that. God's grace is measured through his life and in the lives of all who know him. God's grace reflected by Mike is evident in the faces of Susan and their four incredible children, and it is evident in the people who are associated with Mike.

One bright spot is that in the spring of 2003, Mike and his brother traveled to Kentucky, where a five-mile stretch of U.S. Highway 68 just outside of Bowling Green was dedicated to the honor and memory of their father, State Trooper William Harold Barrett.

For Mike, the world is full of evil and the injury that goes with it. He has tasted some of life's most bitter waters. He admits, "In the years since my dad's death, there have been plenty of opportunities for me to go down in life and blame this tragedy. But God has given me grace and blessed me abundantly, and ultimately, it's His judgment and I have to live with that."

The apostle Paul urges us, "Do not be overcome by evil but overcome evil with good" (Rom. 12:21). Don't waste your sorrows or miss the stewardship of hardship in your life. Life isn't easy; it's a piece of work. But let God work in you and through your struggles to bring grace to others in a time of need.

we are shaped by experiences

*Every experience that God gave us, every person He puts in our lives,
is the perfect preparation for the future only He can see.*

—*Corrie Ten Boom*

Life is a series of experiences that stretch us, try us, grow us, and overwhelm us.

Blessed Are the Flexible

Many, if not most, of life's experiences are beyond our control. They are simply events to which we must respond and adjust. And because life is full of surprises, adjusting is essential.

As we go through life, we are shaped by our family experiences, educational experiences, spiritual experiences, vocational experiences, ministry experiences, and painful or sorrowful experiences. God uses all these experiences to test us, to mature us, and to provide ministry to others through us.

Life Hurts

Romans 12:17 begins with a statement of fact that life hurts. Evil is a "reality show" in life.

Challenge the Principle of Payback

Our world is full of people who have at one time or another been victimized by unjust treatment and undeserved injury. No one gets through unharmed.

In Romans 12, we are provided guidance to deal with our individual responses to the injuries of life.

I will not allow any man to make me lower myself by hating him.
—Booker T. Washington

Concentrate on Doing Good and Keeping Peace

Instead of getting even, we are to focus our attention on getting ahead. The way to get ahead is to stay above the fray of revenge. So instead of getting even, we are instructed to keep peace.

Keeping peace does not mean going easy but taking responsibility to redeem, restore, and make right.

Comfort Your Heart with God's Promise

"'Vengeance is Mine, I will repay,' says the Lord" (Rom. 12:19). God promises revenge. It is a character issue for Him.

Choose the Stewardship of Good over Evil

When injury comes and we experience setbacks in life, we are not to sit back and wait; we are to go forward and walk with God. What are we to do? Work for good.

"Do not be overcome by evil, but overcome evil with good" (Rom. 12:21).

chapter 12
we are called to influence

I voted today. But I'm mad. My candidates didn't lose (well, one did). The political platforms weren't overly controversial. The issue was my precinct. They changed it!

I've voted in each election at the same place for the past four years. Today, Connie and I ventured out early to get the job done. We were at the door at 7 a.m. It was the first order of business in our day. We arrived while the line was still relatively short, only to be greeted with, "I'm sorry; your name isn't in our book."

The volunteer had an antiquated three-ring binder with pages filled with names and addresses of voters in that precinct. Apparently, I'm in another precinct now, but no one is sure where. Connie and I gave our address and location to the volunteer, and one helper suggested that our appropriate precinct location was at a newly constructed middle school several miles to the north. What was intended to be a thirty-minute civic duty was turning out to be an hour-long drudgery.

I decided the simplest solution was to go to the correct voting poll. Connie and I got back in the car and headed to the projected location. When we arrived, we stepped out of the car and onto the campus of a beautiful, efficiently designed, and technically savvy campus.

As we approached the voting area, we quickly realized the outdated voter signage and polling setup did not match the campus. Once again, we approached a table of volunteers who opened three-ring binders and looked for our names. Then it happened—again. "We're sorry; your name is not here. You can't vote in this location."

With a mild tone of frustration, I related our "precinct plight" from the first stop on our pilgrimage of citizenship. By now, I was feeling edgy. Two cups of coffee, no breakfast, a twenty-five-minute drive across town, and a day filled with deadlines were making me feel something other than civil. To make matters worse, I was scheduled to speak at a business luncheon on the subject of "Mouth Management," and my mouth was filled with temptation!

The group of volunteers at the middle school had less information than the first group. They did not have a precinct location finder list or a telephone number. Instead, they shrugged their shoulders and said, "I don't know."

I was now an hour and a half into my day and still hadn't voted. Connie, my lovely, wise, and practical wife, noticed a stack of brochures on the table. She picked one up and found a phone number for voting information. As we walked back to the car, we called for help. Guess what? The proper polling location was two miles south of my original polling stop.

I was fifteen miles north, and by now it was the morning rush hour. My first inclination was to just give up and drive back home. But I didn't. I drove to the correct polling location. I voted. Two hours, a quarter of a tank of gas, and a morning of frustration had me thinking, *No wonder people ignore elections!* But when it was finally over, Connie and I laughed about the memorable experience.

Voting is a huge hassle. But in our society, it is both privilege and responsibility. In fact, citizenship is part of our spiritual stewardship toward God. Our personal engagement in our community is intended to be an expression of our walk with Christ.

Faith and Citizenship

There can be no separation between faith and citizenship. When Jesus Christ changes a person's life, every relationship in that person's life changes. The Christian sees and understands the role of government differently than before. As believers, we recognize that an essential part of citizenship is not only understanding individual rights but also accepting individual responsibilities.

The Word of God gives us insight into the kind of citizens we are to be in regard to the role and relationship we have to government. God has established all authority and delegated it to different realms of life. There are three institutions that have God-ordained and God-established authority and responsibility in our lives: *church*, *home*, and *government*. Our relationship to all three is a reflection of our relationship with God.

Jesus Christ is the foundation of the *church* (1 Cor. 3:11). Upon that foundation, the church of Jesus Christ is to go forward through every generation with the organization and mobilization of apostles, prophets, evangelists, pastors, teachers, and church members. The gates of hell are not to prevail against it (Matt. 16:18).

> When Jesus Christ changes a person's life, every relationship in that person's life changes.

God established the structure of the *home*. The Bible says that God made male and female, assigning to each roles and responsibilities. Children are under the authority of their parents, and parents are to train, nurture, and guide their children.

But what does the Bible teach us concerning *government* and, in particular, citizenship?

Honor the Authority of the State

Government is established by God to serve as an umbrella of justice, righteousness, protection, privacy, and instruction to its citizens. The Bible is very clear that a Christian has a civil responsibility in society.

Throughout history, Christians have taken various positions concerning their role as citizens. Some Christians sought to separate themselves from government, having no involvement or connection with its officials. They avoided service in the military and ignored elections.

Other Christians have been proponents of what I would call subjection of the state. That is, they believed that the church was essentially to overrule the state, taking the place of state and government. There was a period in history where the church-state relationship was unified. In England and Rome, the government ultimately tainted the church, and as a result, the church lost its purity in mission and message.

> **The Bible is very clear that a Christian has a civil responsibility in society.**

Yet the role of religion and the role of government are inseparably woven together for us as believers. It is my firm belief that this understanding provided impetus and growth for the American dream in the foundational years. John Adams, the second U.S. president, understood this balance of power and blend of responsibility when he said, "We have no government armed with power capable of contending with human passions unbridled by morality and religion. Avarice, ambition, revenge or gallantry would break the strongest cords of our Constitution as a whale goes through a net. Our constitution was made only for a moral and religious people. It is wholly inadequate to the government of any other."

Biblically, we should all live in subjection to the authority of government, recognizing that government ultimately answers to the authority of God. By living in subjection to the government as a responsible citizen, you and I are giving testimony of our submission to God. Because our American government is that of a republic functioned through democratic process, our response and responsibility makes this a matter of extreme importance. We all have a stewardship of citizenship.

The apostle Paul urges us to pray for and give thanks for those who have governmental authority over us: "Therefore I exhort first of all that supplications, prayers, intercessions, and giving of thanks be made for all men, for kings and all who are in authority, that we may lead a quiet and peaceable life in all godliness and reverence" (1 Tim. 2:1–2).

And in his letter of instruction to the young pastor Titus, Paul echoes this theme: "Remind them to be subject to rulers and authorities, to obey, to be ready for every good work, to speak evil of no one, to be peaceable, gentle, showing all humility to all men" (Titus 3:1–2).

> To honor our government is to honor our God!

The apostle Peter also understood this truth and taught that believers should submit to the God-ordained authority of the government. He writes, "Therefore submit yourselves to every ordinance of man for the Lord's sake, whether to the king as supreme, or to governors, as to those who are sent by him for the punishment of evildoers and for the praise of those who do good. For this is the will of God, that by doing good you may put to silence the ignorance of foolish men—as free, yet not using liberty as a cloak for vice, but as bondservants of God. Honor all people. Love the brotherhood. Fear God. Honor the king" (1 Pet. 2:13–17).

And finally, the apostle Paul makes his point crystal clear in the book of Romans: "Let every soul be subject to the governing authorities. For there is no authority except from God, and the authorities that exist are appointed by God" (13:1).

When these verses were written, the relationship between believers and the state was anything but tranquil. In fact, the book of Romans was written to believers in Rome, the city most associated with the persecution of the Christian faith. Nero, the infamous emperor of Rome, was consumed with totally annihilating anyone or anything associated with Christians. Yet Paul instructs believers to be subject to the authority of government.

We also learn through the writings of Christians, such as John Foxe's *Book of Martyrs*, that believers throughout history devoted themselves to Christ and His teachings amid great persecution and suffering. Christians were portrayed as government subversives because they would not renounce their faith. Yet they honored the state and its judgments—however misguided—knowing their lives were ultimately under the authority of God.

To honor our government is to honor our God! I believe that is where we can find a basis for patriotism. We can love and honor our country even though we do not fully agree with the government. Although there are many things we condemn in our society, we must understand that ultimately, by honoring government, we are honoring God.

Obey the Laws of the Land

The apostle Paul continues his teaching on the importance of submission to government in Romans 13: "Therefore whoever resists the authority resists the ordinance of God, and those who resist will bring judgment on themselves. For rulers are not a terror to good works, but to evil. Do you want to be unafraid of the authority? Do what is good, and you will have praise from the same" (vv. 2–3).

What if the government does something that God does not approve of in His Word? There's a good example of that situation in the book of Acts. Peter and others had been preaching. They were put in prison, beaten, and told that they could never speak again of Jesus. They made this statement: "We ought to obey God rather than men" (Acts 5:29).

> God honors people who submit in their hearts to the lordship of Jesus Christ, honor the state, and obey the laws of the land.

There could be a situation where a law of government would be in direct violation to the Word of God. In that instance, the Christian has to choose to do what is right by the Word of God.

There are many instances in which the law may either make provision for or provide protection for things to which we are opposed as

Christians. In these cases, we simply need to continue to obey the laws of the land that are right with God and to work to make a difference in the laws that are wrong before God.

God never honors rebellion! God honors people who submit in their hearts to the lordship of Jesus Christ, honor the state, and obey the laws of the land.

Fear the Punishment of Law Enforcement

Paul says about the government officials in authority over us: "For he is God's minister to you for good. But if you do evil, be afraid; for he does not bear the sword in vain; for he is God's minister, an avenger to execute wrath on him who practices evil" (Rom. 13:4).

God has given officials of the state the power to defend the authority of the state. In Romans 13:4, the government's authority is represented by the power of the sword. Today, the power of the policeman's badge and gun is representative of his authority. As citizens, we are to fear the punishment of law enforcement because God has given that responsibility to the state. Criminals are to be held responsible for their crimes under the authority given to the government.

We are not to bear the sword in personal vendettas. Everyone who takes up the sword in rebellion against the state is ultimately a vigilante. The Bible makes it clear that the state has the challenge and obligation of bringing vengeance against every evil within its authority.

In the book of Deuteronomy, God gave Israel the standards of the Law, by which they were to live and to conduct themselves in society. Although most of us are not part of the nation of Israel, the principles by which Israel operated governmentally were the core principles upon which our own government was established. The Founding Fathers of the United States established our government on the provision and the honor of the Ten Commandments. Without these commandments, there is no basis of law by which judgments are made in our courts each day. For this reason, in days gone by, many government facilities were inscribed with statements from the Scripture to recognize the authority of God and the responsibility of the state. The same is acknowledged in our pledge of allegiance.

Let me take a moment to highlight some things that the Bible teaches us on this matter of the objectives of punishment through law enforcement.

Punishment Is to Be Proportionate

Whenever there is a punishment for a crime, it is to be proportionate to the offense. Deuteronomy 19:21 says, "Your eye shall not pity: life shall be for life, eye for eye, tooth for tooth, hand for hand, foot for foot."

The concept behind this command was to provide a statute of limitations so that the punishment against the crime would never be greater than the crime itself. The purpose of law enforcement is to provide punishment that is proportionate to the offense. The punishment is not to exceed the offense.

Punishment Is to Be a Deterrent

The Bible indicates that when people are punished, it is a deterrent to others. Deuteronomy 17:13 relates to the deterrent activity of punishment: "And all the people shall hear and fear, and no longer act presumptuously."

When a strong system of criminal justice not only understands the need for proportionate punishment but also understands that punishment is necessary, the Bible says that punishment is a deterrent.

Punishment Is to Be Impartial

Punishment should never be enforced to favor the rich over the poor or the poor over the rich. Nor should any human relationship have preference over another. Deuteronomy 19:15–21 declares that an accusation must be established by two or three witnesses and that enforcement of penalty is to be done equally and without partiality.

Punishment Is to Be Without Delay

In Deuteronomy 25, we find someone who is before the court and the punishment brought against him. But even more importantly, Ecclesiastes 8:11 tells us, "Because the sentence against an evil work is not executed speedily, therefore the heart of the sons of men is fully set in them to do evil."

> Whenever someone has committed a crime, there is to be punishment without delay.

Whenever punishment does not come quickly, the hearts of people are fully set to do evil. In our society today, we have deferred punishment in the name of "personal rights" to the degree that we have practically destroyed the responsibility of society. Whenever someone has committed a crime, there is to be punishment without delay.

Punishment Is to Focus on Pardon and Restoration

The purpose of punishment is to increase the responsibility of the offender, to deepen the offender's understanding of obligation, and to bring that person back into society without the stigma of the crime (see Deut. 25:3). Isn't it interesting today that no nation in the world has a higher per capita prison inmate population than America? Yet we also have the highest crime rate in the world. The two go hand in hand: many crimes, many criminals.

Our society keeps feeding the system that constantly continues to defer, distract, and absolve criminals rather than focusing on punishment and responsibility and obligation and change. What we are doing is basically creating schools of criminology. We are allowing our prisons to be filled with people who never have to face the responsibility of changing their behavior or being punished for their crimes. As a result, they simply become more sophisticated criminals and they repeat their crimes, often in more heinous ways.

We must understand that whenever a nation does not honor and

administer justice, it will crumble. But let's get back to our stewardship of citizenship.

Make a Positive Contribution to Your Community

The solution to making a positive contribution to your community
is laid out clearly in this chapter of Romans.

First, *pay your taxes*. Isn't that interesting? The Bible says a part of
the solution is that you are to pay your taxes. In Romans 13:6, Paul
says that we are to pay taxes because we are to support the government, that the government might be able to have the resources necessary to keep society secure.

Second, *support your leaders*. Romans 13:7 says that we are to give
honor to whom honor is due. The Bible makes it very clear that even
if we do not respect the person, we are always to honor the position.
There are many times when we do not honor the life or the lifestyle
of the person who holds an office, but we are to honor the position
that person holds. The Bible says
that we are to support our leaders.

Third, *vote your conscience*. The
apostle Paul goes on to say in this
verse that we are to give "custom to
whom customs [are due]." One of
the customs in American life is the

> Whenever a nation
> does not honor and
> administer justice,
> it will crumble.

custom of voting. As we have already discussed, voting is a privilege!
It is a right. But even more than that, as a Christian, it is a responsibility. Every believer needs to take that responsibility seriously, and
we need to vote our conscience.

Most importantly, *love your neighbors*. Far from the rule of law is the
rule of love. For the Christian, the highest rule of life is the rule of
love—a love that cares, a love that takes responsibility. I believe that a
great need in our nation today is for Christians to cover America with
a fresh blanket of love: a love that demonstrates the love of Jesus

Christ, a love of surrender, a love of sacrifice, a love of responsibility, and a love of civility.

Dr. Erwin Lutzer said it well: "One reason the world is so smug in unbelief is that it has lost faith in the believability of God." Most unbelievers have not seen what a credible Christian witness, a true representation of Jesus Christ and God, alive and working, looks like. They have seen angry and judgmental Christians. They have seen many inconsistent Christians. They have seen scandals that have made them wonder if the Christian faith should be dismissed.

> For the Christian, the highest rule of life is the rule of love.

Humanly speaking, there may be powerful reasons that many in our world do not believe today. Jesus said, "By this all will know that you are My disciples, if you have love for one another" (John 13:35). The great rule that needs to be applied to our lives is the rule of love—that we in society would show the love of Jesus Christ!

we are called to influence

Honor the Authority of the State

"Let every soul be subject to the governing authorities. For there is no authority except from God, and the authorities that exist are appointed by God" (Rom. 13:1).

Government is established by God to serve as an umbrella of justice, righteousness, protection, privacy, and instruction to its citizens. The Bible is very clear that a Christian has a civil responsibility in society.

Our constitution was made only for a moral and religious people. It is wholly inadequate to the government of any other.
—John Adams

Obey the Laws of the Land

"Therefore whoever resists the authority resists the ordinance of God, and those who resist will bring judgment on themselves. For rulers are not a terror to good works, but to evil. Do you want to be unafraid of the authority? Do what is good, and you will have praise from the same" (Rom. 13:2–3).

Fear the Punishment of Law Enforcement

"For he is God's minister to you for good. But if you do evil, be afraid; for he does not bear the sword in vain; for he is God's minister, an avenger to execute wrath on him who practices evil. Therefore you must be subject, not only because of wrath but also for conscience' sake" (Rom. 13:4–5).

- Punishment is to be proportionate.
- Punishment is to be a deterrent.
- Punishment is to be impartial.
- Punishment is to be without delay.
- Punishment is to focus on justice and restoration.

Make a Positive Contribution to Your Community

- Pay your taxes.
- Support your leaders.
- Vote your conscience.
- Love your neighbor.

One reason the world is so smug in unbelief is that it has lost faith in the believability of God.
—Dr. Erwin Lutzer

chapter 13
we are entrusted to invest

A little boy was sitting in a church pew. The boy looked up at the usher as he was handing him the offering plate and asked, "Don't you have a child's plate?"

While we are comfortable talking about many other issues of life, the one that always makes us squirm is the matter of money. Why? Money matters. It matters to you. It matters to me. It matters to others. And most importantly, it matters to God.

There was no other matter Jesus Christ addressed more frequently or thoroughly than the issue of money. Time and time again, He made it clear that the condition of our hearts can best be assessed by our use of money. What we do with our money matters. Why?

Money impacts every area of life. Money reflects our values. Money affects our relationships. Money communicates to our children. Money can resource or limit ministry. Money affects health care and retirement. The love of money can corrupt, defile, and twist human lives and hearts. Money is a potent presence and powerful resource.

For these reasons, Jesus did not leave the subject alone. In Mark 12:17, He said, "Render to Caesar the things that are Caesar's, and to God the things that are God's." In this command, Jesus affirmed the responsibility of our individual citizenship and at the same time provided instruction for us as believers to honor God's plan for participation in His work through mission and ministry.

I believe this is a direct reference to our personal stewardship as servants of Christ and responsibility as members of His body, the church.

What Jesus addressed in Mark and numerous other passages in the Gospels is what Paul is emphasizing in Romans 13. Part of the plan for our lives is to handle our personal property and possessions as a trust for God. We are trustees of the treasures God has given us in life. And while you may not think your ship has come in—or

> The condition of our hearts can best be assessed by our use of money.

when your dinghy is being threatened by larger ships in the harbor—God has big plans for us as we learn to partner with and prove Him in the area of our faith and finances.

Let's make some observations about money matters and our money management.

Submit—The Principle of Authority

Our currency reflects something of American history and government. The picture of our first president, George Washington, is at the center point on the dollar bill. In addition to that, there are marks of identification and authenticity on the bill that make them important as a government issue. In fact, if I take a dollar bill and tear it in half, I am liable for destruction of property of the United States government. Whenever you hold a dollar bill, or whatever the face of the denomination may be, it is important that you understand several things.

First, the dollar bill belongs to you. Second, the bill belongs not only to you but to the American government. The government is the owner that issued the bill and established the currency system in our society. And third, the bill belongs to God. You may ask, "How is that true?" It is yours because it came from the mint. It came from the mint because it came from the mine. Our currency is established on a gold and silver exchange. "The silver is Mine, and the gold is Mine,' says the LORD of hosts" (Hag. 2:8).

There is not a dollar bill in circulation that does not ultimately belong to God. All money comes from God. He owns it. But He has established it in a system called government, and in that system we are to live under the authority of God with responsible citizenship. This entire issue of circulation, both in our lives and in our land, is ultimately a part of the responsibility that we have toward God. Therefore, we are to submit to the laws of our state and pay taxes, but we are also to take the money that God has provided and invest it for other purposes. Remember what Jesus taught in Mark 12:17: "Render to Caesar the things that are Caesar's."

> As believers who have experienced new life in Christ, we submit in our money management because of God's authority.

Now let's look at Romans 13:7: "Render therefore to all their due." The word translated "render" is the same word Jesus used in Mark 12. But Jesus goes on to say that we must render "to God the things that are God's." There are two serious issues of submission when it comes to money and our lives. One of those is to the *government* and the other is to *God*.

If you are not faithful to the government through your taxes and you are not faithful to God through your tithe, then you are a rebel. You are worse than a rebel; you are a robber! I dare say that some people drive (even to church) in stolen cars. Some may be wearing clothes that have been stolen. Some may have jewelry that has been stolen because the dollars that were used for their purchase were taken from funds that should be given rightfully to the government, or even more importantly, funds that should be given to God.

Submission is a very important issue. As believers who have experienced new life in Christ, we submit in our money management because of God's authority.

When we see and understand God's authority over our finances, we begin to treat money in a different way. I am like a bank teller who, at the end of the day, must give an account for what has passed through my hands on that day.

Remit—The Principle of Responsibility

Everyone who has ever paid a bill knows that in the front window of that envelope, the bill clearly says "Remit Payment." In other words, you need to return the bill along with a determined amount of money.

As we haves seen, the apostle Paul reminds us, "Render therefore to all their due: taxes to whom taxes are due, customs to whom customs, fear to whom fear, honor to whom honor" (Rom. 13:7).

Every one of us has a responsibility to respond, to do what we are told to do, and to give what we owe. The Bible tells us that we owe two things: taxes and tithes.

Taxes

Your annual responsibility to the Internal Revenue Service can be somewhat more worshipful if you recognize that God has told you to do it. There are penalties imposed by our government if you do not pay your taxes by April 15. Then there are consequences if you continue to refuse to pay the taxes or the penalties after April 15. You can spend a considerable amount of time in jail for tax evasion. Just ask Richard Hatch—the survivor.

Recently, Richard Hatch, who had become a millionaire as the sole "survivor" on the primetime television show bearing that name, was sentenced to fifty-one months in prison. How does a man go from being such a big winner to being such a profiled loser in a few short years? He failed to pay taxes on his earnings. It turns out that surviving at the outpost of Borneo and surviving the Internal Revenue Service are two distinct challenges.

There are severe consequences if you fail or refuse to pay your

taxes, and the penalty of such a failure after April 15 of any given calendar year can be enforced by United States law. God says that He
has established the government, that we have a responsibility toward
the government of paying taxes, and that we will experience consequences if we do not.

Tithes

We are also to tithe to the Lord. What is a tithe? The word *tithe*
means tenth. The first tenth of everything we earn is to be returned
to the Lord.

God has a flat tax. There are no exemptions. You simply take what
you earn and deduct one-tenth. That is God's standard. It is to be
returned to the Lord as an expres-
sion of our understanding that He
is the provider and that we are the
managers of what we have. We are
enriched by God, and in turn we are
to enrich others.

> We are enriched by
> God, and in turn we
> are to enrich others.

We first see the Bible's teaching about the tithe in the book of
Genesis. Abraham paid a tithe, the first tenth of all he had, to
Melchizedek, the king of Salem and a priest (Gen. 14:18–20). The
Bible tells us that even before the time of Moses, the patriarchs paid
tithes, as demonstrated by Abraham and Jacob (Gen. 28:22). In the
books of Leviticus, Deuteronomy, and Numbers, God reminded the
people that they were to tithe and bring the first fruits of their offerings
to the Lord (Lev. 27:30–34; Deut. 14:22–39; Num. 18:20–32).

Not only is the principle of tithing taught in the books of the Law,
but it is clear in both the Major and Minor Prophets. These books
discuss the importance of tithing and the people's failure to meet
God's standard. The prophet Malachi declared, "Will a man rob
God? Yet you have robbed Me! But you say, 'In what way have we
robbed You?' In tithes and offerings.' . . . 'Bring all the tithes into the
storehouse, that there may be food in My house, and try Me now in

this,' says the LORD of hosts, 'If I will not open for you the windows of heaven and pour out for you such blessing that there will not be room enough to receive it," (Mal. 3:8, 10).

And in the New Testament, Jesus confronted the Pharisees with these words:

> "Woe to you, scribes and Pharisees, hypocrites! For you pay tithe of mint and anise and cummin, and have neglected the weightier matters of the law: justice and mercy and faith. These you ought to have done, without leaving the others undone." (Matt. 23:23)

Now when Jesus said, "you pay tithe," He was not criticizing the Pharisees' payment of the tithe; instead, He was affirming it. He then condemned the Pharisees because they had neglected other important things.

In his first letter to the Corinthians, Paul says that believers should set aside an offering at the beginning of the week to give to the Lord (see 1 Cor. 16:3). The tithe came before the Law, and it was affirmed after the Law. The tithe has never been repealed. Some people may believe a New Testament Christian does not have to abide by the tithe described in the Old Testament. However, anyone who would use this as an excuse to give less than the Jews gave under the Law does not understand the message of grace.

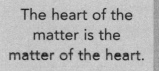

The heart of the matter is the matter of the heart.

Whenever Jesus fulfilled the Old Testament Law, He did not lower the standard; He increased it. For example, the Old Testament said, "You shall not commit adultery." Jesus affirmed the Law and then added, "But I say unto you that whoever looks at a woman to lust for her has already committed adultery with her in his heart" (Matt. 5:28). In other words, the heart of the matter is the matter of the heart.

Someone who fights the idea of the tithe or resists the standard set by the Law will only stumble more with the intent of grace. Jesus raised God's standard; He never lowered it.

In terms of giving, a tenant would never go to his landlord and declare, "Here's how much I want to pay." Instead, a tenant asks the landlord what he has to pay. Likewise, someone borrowing money from a lender does not say, "This is what I'm going to pay and that's it!" If that occurred, the lender would say, "Well, then, you can't have this piece of property." Yet time and time again, it seems that we feel we can establish our own standard of ability and equity when it comes to our response to God in giving. We must begin where God begins, and we can't ignore God's standard in giving.

If you fail to honor the government with your taxes, eventually you are going to be audited. If you do not pass that audit, you are either going to pay large penalty fees or go to jail for tax evasion.

While you ought to give to and support your local church, your church is not going to put you in jail. But do not be deceived into thinking you are not going to be audited by God. As we will examine more fully in the next chapter, "each of us shall give account of himself to God" (Rom. 14:12). There is coming a day of accounting and reckoning for what we have done with what we have received. God has given us a standard for giving.

We have a wonderful benefit in our government: the more we give to charitable causes, the less we pay in taxes. However, I submit to you that if the "charitable contributions" line item on your income tax statement does not significantly reduce the amount of taxes you are paying or does not reflect a tenth of what you have made, then the IRS may have just given you a clear picture of your true spiritual condition.

Commit—The Principle of Charity

Let's continue with our reflections on money matters by considering another of the challenges Paul places before us: "Owe no one anything except to love one another, for he who loves another has fulfilled the law" (Rom. 13:8).

This verse is often misinterpreted as a prohibition against the use of debt. This could not be further from the truth! Living out of debt is a good principle, but that is not what is being taught in this passage. The Bible is telling us that when we fail to meet our obligation to the government, we fail to do what we should do to our fellow man. Consequently, we are stealing from society, cheating the government, and robbing ourselves. Ultimately, we are robbing God.

> The motivating force of our life should not be the love of money.

Imprinted on every dollar bill in America are these words: "This note is legal tender for all debts public and private." You can settle financial debts in your life, but the Bible says there is a debt that comes from above that you cannot settle with money. It is the debt of love that we owe to others.

The motivating force of our life should not be the love of money. In fact, the Bible says that "the love of money is a root of all kinds of evil" (1 Tim. 6:10). But to the contrary, the great love of our hearts is to be a love for people, because people need the Lord. We have a debt of love that we owe to everyone.

The hymn writer Isaac Watts said it well when he penned these words:

> But drops of grief can ne'er repay
> The debt of love I owe;
> Here, Lord, I give myself away,
> 'Tis all that I can do.

Since we have been set free and forgiven by Jesus Christ and the great payment of His cross, our hearts' desire is to be faithful to Him in all areas of our lives. The debt of our lives is to be a channel of love for others to know Jesus Christ. When that is not the motivating force of all of our giving, then we have missed the whole purpose of Christian living. It is all about the love of Jesus Christ!

> God is inviting us into the greatest joy and privilege in the world: to become a partner with Him.

When it comes to our possessions, God's goal for us is not our checkbooks, our bank accounts, or our credit lines. God's goal is to get to our hearts—not acting out of obligation but out of love for Jesus Christ! If God does not do something in our hearts and change the motivation of why we do what we do, then we will never amount to anything spiritually as a people, a church, or individual Christians. We need to be moved by the Spirit of love. God is inviting us into the greatest joy and privilege in the world: to become a partner with Him.

The Lasting Impact of a Life Invested

Standing at the doorway of a church gymnasium in Memphis, Tennessee, my dad asked the worn and weary man if he would like a hot shower and a warm meal. Hours earlier, the man had traveled more than four hundred miles north from the Gulf Coast, which had been ravaged by Hurricane Katrina. His house had collapsed on top of him, and he had to swim out to safety.

Each mile he traveled this day was a reminder that the life he lived and the place he called home would never be the same. At his age and stage of life, even the most aggressive efforts to rebuild could not recover the lifetime he had lost through such a devastating storm.

The weary traveler thanked my father for his offer and headed toward the shower. When he emerged a few minutes later, dripping wet, he looked bewildered. He didn't have to say a word. Dad asked him gently, "You don't have a shirt, do you?"

The old man admitted, "All I have left in this world are the clothes

I wore in the door." His voice broke as he realized the totality of his personal loss. With trembling voice in return, Dad asked, "What color shirt would you like?" The man replied, "Mister, I am at your mercy. I don't have anything." Dad walked the man out the door of the church toward his car.

As Dad opened the trunk of the car, he could hardly contain his joy. Before leaving the house that warm September morning, Dad had gone to his closet and taken a pile of clothes. He thought he might add them to the goods being gathered at the church for hurricane evacuees. He never dreamed he would have such a personal encounter with a man who so desperately needed a shirt.

The man chose a blue dress shirt. Clean and freshly clothed, there they stood: one was a fisherman, the other a retired salesman. A tragedy introduced these two men, but a gift made them friends.

I was standing in the international terminal at the airport when I spoke with Dad by phone. It was my last call before boarding a flight headed to Romania. I called to tell Dad I loved him. I wanted to let him know I would be back in touch once we arrived and were settled in the city of Brailia for a three-day pastors' conference.

Dad told me in a broken voice about his introduction moments earlier to this needy old man. He told me about the shirt and the tears of joy. He didn't have to say any more. The gift and the giver had been touched and used.

I was so proud of my dad. I was grateful for the heart of service and concern for others I had witnessed in him over a lifetime. I could tell his life had been impacted by the storm as well, but the impact was one I never wanted to forget.

> It is one of the greatest of all life's lessons: when you learn to give, you learn to live.

As I boarded my plane, I was smiling inside. I kept reflecting on the tone of Dad's voice and the words he shared: "What color shirt would you like?" My dad had just given a man he barely knew one of the most needed gifts the man had ever received. Dad took a shirt on a hanger and turned it into a covering of loving comfort for a man who needed a shirt and so much more.

I didn't get to see any of this happen. It wasn't recorded for a future feature or human-interest story. But standing in an airport nearly five hundred miles away, I felt the impact of Dad's generous impulse. I shared the joy of giving. My heart was soaring before my plane left the ground.

It is one of the greatest of all life's lessons: when you learn to give, you learn to live.

If you are not giving, you are robbing yourself of what God could and would do in your life. Jesus said, "For what will it profit a man if he gains the whole world, and loses his own soul?" (Mark 8:36).

You will never want what you get if you try to get all you want in life. Learn this simple truth: the life you were born to live is the life you were born to give.

we are entrusted to invest

One of the greatest missing teachings in the American church today is the reminder to men and women that nothing we have belongs to us.

—Gordon MacDonald

Money impacts every area of life. Money reflects our values. Money impacts our relationships. Money communicates to our children. Money can resource or limit ministry. Money affects health care and retirement. The love of money can corrupt, defile, and twist human lives and hearts. Money is a potent presence and powerful resource.

Submit—The Principle of Authority

A dollar bill may belong to you, but it also belongs to the government. The government issued the bill and established the currency system in our society. And, of course, the bill belongs to God.

God has established the dollar bill in a system called government, and in that system of government, we are to live under the authority of God with responsible citizenship.

"'The silver is Mine, and the gold is Mine,' says the LORD of hosts" (Hag. 2:8).

Remit—The Principle of Responsibility

Taxes: God says that He has established the government, that we have a responsibility toward the government to pay taxes, and that we will experience consequences if we do not.

Tithes: "Will a man rob God? Yet you have robbed Me! But you say, 'In what way have we robbed You?' In tithes and offerings. . . . 'Bring all the tithes into the storehouse, that there may be food in My house, and try Me now in this,' says the LORD of hosts, 'If I will not open for you the windows of heaven and pour out for you such blessing that there will not be room enough to receive it'" (Mal. 3:8, 10).

"So then each of us shall give account of himself to God" (Rom. 14:12).

Commit—The Principle of Charity

"Owe no one anything except to love one another, for he who loves another has fulfilled the law" (Rom. 13:8).

Since we have been set free and forgiven by Jesus Christ and the great payment of His cross, our hearts' desire is to live a life faithful to Him in all areas. The debt of our lives is to be a channel of love for others to know Jesus Christ. When that is not the motivating force of all our giving, then we have missed the whole purpose of Christian living. It is all about the love of Jesus Christ!

"For what will it profit a man if he gains the whole world, and loses his own soul?" (Mark 8:36).

chapter 14
we are tested by time

I heard about a waitress who worked at a roadside restaurant. She got so tired of people always asking, "What time is it?" that she placed a large digital clock on top of the cash register. People stopped asking about the time, but to her dismay, they replaced that question with another: "Is that clock right?"

My friend and gifted communicator Charles Lowery talks about our obsession with time in this way:

"In our communication we have instant messaging, at mealtime we have fast food, for our car care there is Jiffy Lube, if you have to cook at home there is Minute Rice, after any big event there is one-hour photo, and almost everywhere you can find drive-thru service." He goes on to say, "Even when you get a break and have time to relax and take a swim, what do you wear? A Speedo!"[1]

We live in a world that is highly time conscious.

Recently, *24* became a hit television series. In this show, viewers observe Special Agent Jack Bauer as he experiences the drama, conflict, and intensity of a life aimed at saving the world. The entire season unfolds one episode at a time, progressing through a single twenty-four-hour day. The pace and pressure of each moment builds as the clock is ticking, the plot is thickening, and anxiety is increasing through the urgency and importance of Jack's mission.

For the Christian, there is a real-life drama unfolding as God works in time and for eternity.

What Does the Bible Say about Time?

The Bible teaches three critical facts about the subject of time. Paul addresses believers about the importance of life management and time focus. But before I get to Paul's words in Romans 13, I want to remind you of several things the Bible teaches concerning time.

God Created Time

In Genesis we read, "So the evening and the morning were the first day" (1:5). Since God is eternal—in other words, He has always been and He will always be—He is not constrained by time. However, He created us to live within a twenty-four-hour day.

God Controls Time

In the book of Joshua, we find an intense battle scene involving the children of Israel. Instead of the sun setting and Joshua losing ground that day, the sun stood still so that the battle could continue until Israel won (Josh. 10:13). And in Galatians 4:4, we learn that Jesus came into this world in "the fullness of the time." There was a countdown on the clock of God's redemptive episode. God synchronized Jesus's birth to just the right moment in history. Also, in Hebrews 9:27, we find that "it is appointed for men to die once, but after this the judgment." In other words, you and I have a scheduled date with destiny. For this reason, the Psalmist prayed, "Teach us to number our days, / That we may gain a heart of wisdom" (Ps. 90:12).

> We live in a world that is highly time conscious.

God Compares Time

In heaven, we will stand before the Lord and reflect on our earthly lives: how we lived, how we managed our time, and what we did with the life God gave to us (see 1 Cor. 3:10–15).

With this understanding, Paul writes in Romans 13:11–14, challenging our influence in society and our service in God's church: "And do this, knowing the time, that now it is high time to awake out of sleep; for now our salvation is nearer than when we first believed. The night is far spent; the day is at hand. Therefore let us cast off the works of darkness, and let us put on the armor of light. Let us walk properly, as in the day, not in revelry and drunkenness, not in lewdness and lust, not in strife and envy. But put on the Lord Jesus Christ, and make no provision for the flesh, to fulfill its lusts."

> For the Christian, there is a real-life drama unfolding as God works in time and for eternity.

The Battleground of Our Time

Paul is writing in this passage as though he were addressing a group of soldiers. During the daylight hours, the soldiers fought courageously in battle. But when darkness covered their camp, the celebration often turned into a drunken party.

Recently, my friend Pat Williams sent me a copy of a book written to fathers entitled *The Warrior Within*. As I read, I was fascinated by a story he told about General George Washington. Pat is an excellent writer, so I want you to read the story as he presented it:

In December 1776, the fate of America hung by the slimmest of threads. General George Washington's makeshift army had suffered a series of humiliating and costly battlefield defeats. . . . His forces shrunk from 17,000 to a mere 3,000 exhausted and underfed men, some without coats or shoes to protect them from the harsh winter. When the Continental Congress in Philadelphia learned that General Washington had retreated to a place just 12 miles away, they panicked and fled to Baltimore, 100 miles to the south. From his camp near the Falls of Trenton, a dispirited General Washington wrote his brother John, "I think the game is pretty near up."

Washington needed a victory. One more battlefield loss and his army would be disbanded. His last hope—and America's— lay across the Delaware River in the sleepy town of Trenton, New Jersey.

The town was guarded by Hessian mercenaries—soldiers imported from Germany to fight for the British. The Hessians were commanded by Colonel Johann Gottlieb Rall, a vile, hard-drinking man without conscience or honor. During the battle in New York, Colonel Rall had ordered his soldiers to slaughter surrendering Americans.

General Washington gambled that the poorly disciplined Hessians would be so hungover after celebrating Christmas that Trenton would fall into his hands like an overripe plum. On Christmas day, Washington divided his meager forces into three units. Washington would lead the largest group, roughly 2,000 men across the Delaware at McKonkey's Ferry, nine miles north of Trenton. The other two groups would cross the river at points further south. As Washington and his men marched toward McKonkey's Ferry, some wore rags in the place of boots. Their footsteps left a trail of blood.

The crossing of the river began at two in the afternoon. It took 14 hours to move all of Washington's men, horses and light cannons across the Delaware. A heavy sleet storm and large ice floes made the passage treacherous and miserable. It was well after 3 A.M. when the entire force was finally safe on the New Jersey side.

A British loyalist spotted Washington's army and sent a

handwritten warning by messenger to the Hessians. The messenger hurried to Trenton and delivered the message to Colonel Rall. The colonel, who was playing cards with his aides, tucked the message into his pocket without reading it.

Meanwhile General Washington rode at the head of his troops on a nine-mile march toward Trenton. Unfortunately, most of his soldiers' muskets had been soaked by the storm. Although a few infantrymen still had dry powder for their guns, most would have to attack with bayonets alone.

Washington's army reached Trenton at 8 A.M., catching the Hessian guards drunk and sleeping at their posts. Riding out in the front of his troops, General Washington shouted, "March on, my brave fellows! After me!" And he turned his horse and led his men into the thick of battle.

Hearing shouts and gunfire, an astonished Colonel Rall staggered out into the streets. "What is this?" he shouted in German. Moments later, he was felled by a gunshot. His men carried him into the Queen Street Methodist Church, where he died. One of his men noticed the corner of a note sticking out of the colonel's pocket. The man opened the note and it read, The American army is marching on Trenton.

The Hessians took heavy losses—more than 200 dead and wounded—and quickly surrendered. The Americans suffered only 4 casualties and took nearly 1,000 Hessians prisoners. The course of the war was completely changed that day, and America exists as a free nation because of George Washington's daring gambit at Trenton.[2]

Know the time. It's time to be awake and alert. Paul says life is a battleground and we must keep watch, stay alert, and be prepared. The battle is sure to come in the morning. There is urgency to the task. There is intensity to living. Don't be caught living carelessly or lethargically. The hour is coming when you will need to be dressed in your armor, ready for battle.

So how should we use the time we have? How can we be good stewards of the gift of life?

Value Time

Paul begins with a challenge in Romans 13:11: "Now it is high time to awake out of sleep; for now our salvation is nearer than when we first believed." It is time to wake up! God has given you today. Don't waste it, squander it, or misuse it. Don't fool around in the dark. God has given you opportunity.

> Time is much more valuable than money.

Why is time so important? It is because time is a limited resource. You have only a certain amount of time on earth. Thomas Edison, the great inventor, said, "Time is the most important thing in the world." Benjamin Franklin, the great forefather of our nation, said, "Dost thou love life? Then do not squander time, for it's the stuff that life is made of."

Have you ever stopped to think about the terms we use to describe time? We say things like *spending time, saving time,* and *investing time.* Spending. Saving. Investing. Sound familiar? Don't we say the same words in reference to money? Money is a tangible expression of values and priorities. Nothing demonstrates who you really are from the heart more than the way you use your money.

However, while money is tangible, time is more valuable. What do I mean? If you have thirty years to live, you can make a million dollars. But if you have only thirty minutes to live, a million dollars doesn't really matter. Time is much more valuable than money.

Balance Time

A critical part of life is learning what it means to balance your time. I addressed this topic in my book *The Search for Satisfaction* by focusing on the ticking of the time clock in Ecclesiastes 3.[3] In this chapter, Solomon tells us that there is an appointed time for everything under heaven. There is a time to be born, a time to die, a time to love, and so on. It is interesting to note that this passage of Scripture gives us the two extremes.

Nothing will give you a greater sense of being out of balance than not handling your time rightly. Not long ago, I was driving my wife's car. I noticed that when I got to a certain speed, the whole front end of the car would shake. I took it to a garage and learned the car was out of balance. It was amazing how much more smoothly it drove once the wheels were rotated and balanced.

> A life out of balance makes for a shaky ride!

In the same way, a life out of balance makes for a shaky ride! So how do we get an unbalanced life in balance?

Devote Time to Worship

The Bible teaches us that God made us to worship Him, and God Himself indicated that man was to take a day and set it aside to put his eyes on the Lord. I can worship God anytime, anywhere, any day, and in a number of ways.

But God also intends worship to be an experience shared with other believers. Some neglect this essential practice and opt instead for private worship on their own terms, without public gathering. However, the writer of Hebrews challenges believers to go on in faith by regularly participating in corporate worship. "So let's do it—full of belief, confident that we're presentable inside and out. Let's keep a firm grip on the promises that keep us going. He always keeps his word. Let's see how inventive we can be in encouraging love and helping out, not avoiding worshiping together as some do but spurring each other on, especially as we see the big Day approaching" (Heb. 10:25 MSG).

We maintain strength, focus, and balance in life when we make time for personal worship and take time to gather with other believers to do the same.

Devote Time to Work

The Bible teaches that every one of us should work. Work is an important part of life. We need to work! In his letter to the Colossian church, the apostle Paul gives valuable instruction about our work: "Whatever you do, do it heartily, as to the Lord and not to men" (Col. 3:23). So when you are doing your job, the Bible says you are to worship God by doing your work in a way that honors the Lord.

> The Bible says you are to worship God by doing your work in a way that honors the Lord.

When God gave Moses the Ten Commandments, He made sure to remind the people to be faithful at work. The Fourth Commandment begins, "Six days you shall labor and do all your work" (Exod. 20:9).

When God said that we should work six days, I am not sure He necessarily meant that you should work at your job six days a week. There is a lot of other work that has to be done, such as housework and yard work. Yet one of the greatest places where people get out of balance is in the area of their work.

The Bible balances our compulsion with this reminder: "It is in vain that you rise up early / and go late to rest, / eating the bread of anxious toil; / for he gives to his beloved sleep" (Ps. 127:2 ESV).

Devote Time to Sleep

Sleep is a necessary part of life. Today, sleep deprivation seems to be the norm and, for far too many people, a badge of true courage. Frankly, depriving yourself of sleep is a sure way to a bed of injury and illness.

According to sleep experts at the University of California, San Diego Medical Center, when we are sleepy, our brains have to work harder and accomplish much less. Our language centers shut down. Our propensity for misjudgment and accidents increases at an alarming rate. In summary, the study concludes: "When it becomes less responsive with sleeplessness, there is not a brain system available to come online to compensate for the negative effects of sleep deprivation."[4] Sleep is essential for physical recovery and, therefore, is indispensable for balance and effectiveness in life. For many of us, getting enough sleep might be the most spiritual thing that we could do.

Devote Time to Family

Family time is essential. One thing the Bible makes very clear is that God has established the order and the priority of the family. Outside of the relationship you have with Christ and with your church, nothing is more important in your life than the relationship you have with your family.

Connie and I have built a significant part of our marriage on coffee and walking. When we get up in the mornings, we spend time together drinking coffee, talking, sharing, and taking a walk together. While I do a lot of things each day, there is nothing more important to me every day than spending that time alone with my wife and being sure that she is plugged into my life and I am plugged into her life. We are walking through life together so that we might be able to live for Jesus Christ.

> For many of us, getting enough sleep might be the most spiritual thing that we could do.

I fight the same struggles you do in trying to find time to focus on my children and to find a balance between quality time and quantity time. I have learned you cannot separate the two. You often hear someone say, "I'm going to give my kids an hour of quality time." Forget it! You cannot segment your lives that way. You cannot schedule quality time to happen. What you can do is give your children a quantity of your time, and in the process, quality will come.

Devote Time to Fun

It is biblical to have fun and laugh. Do you think God gave us our laughter any less than He gave us our tears? God gave us our tears to express our grief, and God gave us our laughter to express our joy. Solomon wisely wrote, "A merry heart does good, like medicine" (Prov. 17:22). You need the medicine of laughter in your life.

As I write these words, I am looking at a picture on my desk of two dear and special friends, John and Charlotte West. I've heard John say on many occasions, "Laughter is the lotion for the sunburns of life." John should know because when he is in the room, lotion is being spread all around.

John is a handsome man who lost his hair at an early age. One time, John and I visited someone at a hospital. The elevator door opened, we entered, and as the door closed, the fun began. John said, "Hi, how are you?" to another traveler on the elevator. As the person responded, "Fine, how are you?" John said, "Terrible. I was on my way in the door, and a gust of wind took my hairpiece right off my head. I had to chase it down the street, and it ended up in a pool of water. And did it ever stink!" Well, you can imagine the shock and the smiles as John carried on his tall tale. But you have to admit, it beats a silent elevator ride!

On another occasion, Connie and I were living in Florida and traveling through Texas on our way out west. It had been a while since we had been with John and Charlotte, so we called and they came out to see us at the airport as we passed through. As we were preparing to board for the second half of our flight, John stood up in the midst of the crowd at the airport and said loudly, "May I have your attention! These are my friends, Connie and David McKinley. They have just gotten married and are off on their honeymoon. Y'all treat them real nice!" Were we embarrassed? You bet! And what made matters worse were the number of people who spoke words of congratulations during the flight. Today, Connie and I still have a great laugh when reflecting on that experience.

Devote Time to Service

A balanced life involves serving other people. Jesus said He "did not come to be served, but to serve, and to give His life a ransom for many" (Matt. 20:28). What was true of Jesus is to be true of his followers. While the slogan WWJD (What Would Jesus Do?) has waned in recent years in its prominence in the Christian marketplace, the relevance of being a servant like Christ has for us has not.

I recently attended a luncheon where my friend Mike Fechner, a Dallas businessman turned community servant and minister for Christ, received the Legends of Service Award given by the Dallas Life Foundation for his sacrifice and investment in addressing the needs of undereducated, underprivileged, and sometimes undesirable people groups in our community. Several years ago, Mike was a hard-charging, high-achieving businessman with strong earnings and increased comforts—

> A balanced life involves serving other people.

until he met a woman named Velma Mitchell. Velma lived in the projects. She faced several points of hardship in her life but none greater than the one that molded her friendship with Mike.

Mike met Velma and her seventeen-year-old son at a community gathering held at our church prior to Thanksgiving that year. Within a few months of the event that facilitated their acquaintance, Velma's teenage son became the victim of a random drive-by shooting. The event broke Mike's heart and changed his life. Mike stopped to reevaluate his life priorities and the emptiness of acquisition without greater stewardship in his life.

As a result, he began to pour his time, energy, and resources into establishing a ministry to inner-city Dallas called Bridge Builders.

Over the next decade-and-a-half, thousands of meals; projects; dental, eye, and medical exams; courses; and jobs were provided, and a fantastic community center has been built because of a defining moment that transformed a heart driven to succeed to become the heart of a servant. And through Mike's service, he and scores of others are now succeeding in life in a whole new dimension.

Devote Time to Reflect

Every one of us needs time to get alone personally and privately with God to nurture our relationship with Him and to consider the direction of our life in light of His plan. We should begin every day with an upward look before an outward look. It was Abraham Lincoln who once said that if he were ever given eight hours to chop down a tree, he would spend the first six hours sharpening the ax.

The Psalmist says, "Be still, and know that I am God" (Ps. 46:10). We all need to pull aside and pull apart at times. As evangelist Vance Havner used to say, "You must come apart, or you will come apart."

Someone has written:

> I met God in the morning
> When my day was at its best,
> And His Presence came like sunrise,
> like a glory in my breast.
>
> All day long the Presence lingered,
> All day long He stayed with me,
> And we sailed in perfect calmness
> O'er a very troubled sea.
>
> Other ships were blown and battered,
> Other ships were sore distressed,

But the winds that seemed to drive them,
Brought to me a peace and rest.

Then I thought of other mornings
With a keen remorse of mind,
When I too had loosed the moorings
With the Presence left behind.

So I think I've learned the secret,
Learned from many a troubled way:
You must seek Him in the morning
If you want Him through the day.[5]

Each element on this list has a different level of importance and a different time sequence. But every one has to be segmented in your life. While they are not equal in priority or in proportion, they are critical to living life on purpose and in balance.

> Don't try to manage your time alone; ask God to help you.

Charles Hummel, author of *The Tyranny of the Urgent*, said, "Our greatest danger in life is permitting the urgent things to crowd out the important things."[6]

Manage Time

Here are some ideas to help you manage your time more effectively. How can we do the important?

Seek God's Help

Don't try to manage your time alone; ask God to help you. He will teach you to listen to His voice. You need to be led by Him every day.

Use a Calendar or Planner

Today, there are numerous devices to help you stay organized. Select something that works for you, and block out what is essential before you schedule everything else. For example, attending church should not be something you decide on Saturday night or Sunday morning. If you wait until the last minute to make that decision, I can tell you what is going to win: the covers, the sheets, and the pillow.

Gather the Fragments

I am convinced that much of life is lost in the fragments of time, not in the slices. These are the small pieces of your life. Several years ago, I began the discipline of journaling. I determined that I would write a page and a half in my journal each day—and it's a small page! I am amazed many years later at how many volumes I have written about my life and what I have walked through and learned. I would never have sat down and written all of that otherwise.

Another way to make use of your fragments of time is to learn to carry a book with you and take five minutes to read. As you stand in line or wait in a parking lot, take an article with you that you have been intending to read. Gather the fragments.

Don't Procrastinate

Mark Twain once quipped, "Don't put off until tomorrow what you can put off until the day after tomorrow." But the Bible says, "Do not boast about tomorrow, / For you do not know what a day may bring forth" (Prov. 27:1). An important part of balancing your life is knowing what your priority is today.

Time Well Spent

When my son, Joseph, was in the fifth grade, he would often come home with L.Q. scribbled at the top of his page. When I first saw it, I wondered what it meant: Late Quiz? Lots of Questions?

Lowest Quadrant of the class? I wasn't sure then, but now I will never forget.

L.Q. represented a review by his teacher, whose name was Doris LaQuire (thus the L.Q.). She was an incredible teacher. She was interesting, animated, and informative. She had a teaching gene that made her classroom infectious. Throughout the year, I watched Joseph thrive in this fertile learning environment, and I observed the same thing with his fellow fifth-graders.

On one occasion, L.Q. sent a formal invitation to my office requesting that the pastor and his wife join the fifth-grade class for "tea." We readily agreed. Several weeks later, we found ourselves in a standard elementary classroom— art on the walls, maps at the front, projects on the counters, desks all around. But on this day, the desks and all of the other fifth-graders' possessions were pushed to the walls, with only a few chairs remaining in a semicircle. A table had been converted to a service area covered with a fine linen tablecloth and china.

> An important part of balancing your life is knowing what your priority is today.

The students were in Sunday dress rather than their usual school uniforms. Tea and tasty treats were served as we were shown to our seats of honor. The students provided special attention as they served us. It was a beautiful, formal, and delightful event. Frankly, I was trying not to drop or spill anything so as not to create a blunder in a moment when we were being shown such honor. After we enjoyed several readings, some questions were directed to us to stimulate mature conversation.

Then we came to the final question. "Pastor and Mrs. McKinley, do you like to have fun?"

I smiled. "Of course!" And with that—before I could respond further—each student lifted a can of silly string from hidden locations and gleefully began to spray. Three colors of fluorescent string covered our heads, hands, and feet. The formal dignity of the moment had turned into a free-for-all, and the laughter and humor changed everything. I had been set up! L.Q. turned her entire fifth-grade class loose, and they charged ahead with full abandon.

I can still hear the children's laughter and see L.Q.'s face as she looked on with great satisfaction. We went from formal tea to all-out war. What a moment!

L.Q. knew that learning, laughter, love, and leadership are inseparable qualities for creating an effective educational environment.

Joseph was only one of several hundred students who shared this fifth-grade experience with Doris LaQuire. Like any classroom of students, his classmates came from many different backgrounds. They all had a variety of talents and gifts, strengths and weaknesses. Yet in the midst of all this diversity was one inspiring teacher: L.Q.

You can only imagine the shock and sadness I felt three years later when I received a call informing me that L.Q. had been diagnosed with a severe and life-threatening form of leukemia.

Doris LaQuire died within a month of the diagnosis. She was forty-two. She lived alone—with the exception of her pugs—and without a lot of earthly notoriety or possessions. However, she did have the love and admiration of her fellow teachers, faculty, and administration. And her church was filled with families who thought she hung the moon.

None of us knew in those days that Doris was living with limited time. But she made the most of it. She didn't squander her life. She didn't pout about things that weren't what she might want or hope for them to be. She simply gave the best of herself—first to the Lord and then to a classroom of fifth-graders who will never forget the influence of her life.

For us, L.Q. represents time well spent. In our hearts and the hearts of all who knew her, L.Q. will always remind us of Doris and her "love quotient."

we are tested by time

The best use of life is to invest it in something which will outlast life.
—William James

What Does the Bible Say about Time?

In the Bible, we are told that:
• God created time.
• God controls time.
• God calculates time.

The Battleground of Our Time

Paul says life is a battleground and we must keep watch, stay alert, and be prepared. Don't be caught living carelessly or lethargically. The hour is coming when you will need to be dressed in your armor, ready for battle.

Value Time

Time is the most important thing in the world.
—Thomas Edison

Dost thou love life? Then do not squander time, for it's the stuff that life is made of.
—Benjamin Franklin

God has given you today. Don't waste it, squander it, or misuse it. Don't fool around in the dark. God has given you opportunity.

Balance Time

• Devote time to worship.
• Devote time to work.
• Devote time to sleep.
• Devote time to your family and building healthy relationships.
• Devote time to fun.
• Devote time to service.
• Devote time to reflect.

Reflection can make experience educational. Reflection can recharge your energies.
"Be still, and know that I am God" (Ps. 46:10).

Our greatest danger in life is permitting the urgent things to crowd out the important things.
—Charles Hummel,
The Tyranny of the Urgent

Manage Time

• Seek God's help.
• Use a calendar or planner.
• Gather the fragments.
• Don't procrastinate.

chapter 15
we are liberated to live responsibly

I have a confession to make: I love steak! Filet. T-bone. Ribeye. New York strip. Chop steak. Hamburger. I love it all! I have an inward bent toward eating meat. However, my outward bulge tells me that I can't eat high volumes of it and the other foods I like without a price.

But to this day, a good grilled steak—medium rare, accompanied by a fresh Caesar salad, a piping-hot baked potato loaded with butter and sour cream, and a warm basket of buttered bread—makes for a feast. Not long ago, I heard someone say while many think the secret to the fountain of youth is extra virgin olive oil, the real secret is butter! Probably not the best medical advice, but it's something many of us can relate to.

When it comes to not eating meat, and steak in particular, it is really a matter of calories rather than character for me. It is much more a matter of health than holiness.

However, there was a day when the simple issue of eating meat was a major issue in the life of the church. In particular, it was a major issue for the Christians who lived in the cities of Rome and Corinth, where meat was plentiful due to pagan worship. The choicest meat was brought to the pagan temples for public sacrifice and celebration.

Among believers in this day, there was one group of people who didn't eat meat because it had been defiled through idol worship. Another group felt they could eat all the meat they wanted because it was something that they could receive with thanksgiving. Which group was right?

In the book of Romans, Paul addressed this issue and provided principles for guidance, ways of helping first-century believers balance faith and practice. Each principle called for a view of life and faith that focused on celebrating liberty in Christ and living responsibly toward other believers as well as the unbelieving world.

As he introduces the debate over whether believers were free to eat or compelled to abstain from meat that had been sacrificed to idols, Paul writes:

> Receive one who is weak in the faith, but not to disputes over doubtful things. For one believes he may eat all things, but he who is weak eats only vegetables. Let not him who eats despise him who does not eat, and let not him who does not eat judge him who eats; for God has received him. Who are you to judge another's servant? To his own master he stands or falls. Indeed, he will be made to stand, for God is able to make him stand. One person esteems one day above another; another esteems every day alike. Let each be fully convinced in his own mind. He who observes the day, observes it to the Lord; and he who does not observe the day, to the Lord he does not observe it. He who eats, eats to the Lord, for he gives God thanks; and he who does not eat, to the Lord he does not eat, and gives God thanks. For none of us lives to himself, and no one dies to himself. For if we live, we live to the Lord; and if we die, we die to the Lord. Therefore, whether we live or die, we are the Lord's. For to this end Christ died and rose and lived again, that He might be Lord of both the dead and the living. . . . So then each of us shall give account of himself to God. (Rom. 14:1–9, 12)

In this portion of his letter to the Romans, Paul addresses an issue of cultural extremes concerning what to eat and not to eat. In this discussion, he provides some important principles for every generation in discerning and deciding how to balance liberty and responsibility.

The issue goes far beyond the matter of meat. The liberty we have as Americans is not a liberty in which everyone does what is right in his or her own eyes. The purpose of having liberty is to live responsibly for the welfare and the benefit of everyone else. The tragedy of our times is the indulgence of right at the expense of responsibility and the welfare of others. With this lacking in our nation, our courts become battlegrounds for civil liberties that exaggerate individual rights above national, moral, and social welfare.

> The purpose of having liberty is to live responsibly for the welfare and the benefit of everyone else.

But that's another subject. Let's get back to Paul and the meat market. As the apostle discusses this subject under the leadership of the Holy Spirit, he introduces the topic with a broad and overarching principle. It is a theme he has been developing throughout the book of Romans and has to do with the depth and height of God's grace and forgiveness found in Christ.

The Principle of Spiritual Liberty

In chapter 8, Paul highlights and celebrates the freedom we have in Jesus Christ from the corruption and condemnation of sin. "There is therefore now no condemnation to those who are in Christ Jesus, who do not walk according to the flesh, but according to the Spirit. For the law of the Spirit of life in Christ Jesus has made me free from the law of sin and death" (Rom. 8:1–2).

In other words, Paul is saying that Jesus fulfilled the Law in every part for us. Therefore, we no longer live under the Law. Now when the Bible says that we have been set free in Christ, this freedom does not for one moment indicate that we have been set free from the moral standards of the Old Testament Law, as I discussed in an earlier chapter.

Jesus took the Ten Commandments and increased them exponentially when He said that if you hate your brother, it is the equivalent of having murder in your heart. He also said that if a man even looks at a woman with lust, he has committed adultery in his heart. Jesus did not lower God's moral standards; He clarified and extended them. And there's more: Jesus fulfilled God's complete and perfect requirement for us.

In *The Search for Satisfaction*, I conclude with the simple yet profound reality that Jesus satisfies.[1] The first and most important of all things Jesus has satisfied is the righteous requirement of a holy God. We cannot rise to the occasion of obedience or God's righteousness in order to come to God of our own effort or merit. But what is impossible for us is possible through Christ.

> Once we receive Jesus Christ as our Savior and Lord, He frees us from the condemnation of sin and takes our lives to another level.

Once we receive Jesus Christ as our Savior and Lord, He frees us from the condemnation of sin and takes our lives to another level. He raises the standards of God to the degree that the only way that we can ever become what God desires and expects is through the power of the Holy Spirit. The Holy Spirit enables us to live a life of purity to God.

Legalism and Liberalism

While Christ has set us free from the condemnation of sin and has given us His Spirit that we might be empowered to live, there are two ditches many believers fall into.

The first ditch is *legalism*—that is, living with a list of rules. The result is that we measure our own spiritual progress by the number of rules we know and enforce, and we measure the progress or maturity of others by our self-imposed standards. The curse of legalism is absorption in things external. There is often outward conformity without inward reality or transformation. And then legalism tries to bring everyone else under the confines of a list of rules.

The Pharisees have become synonymous with this in the New Testament. They were not all a corrupt crowd. They were respected. They were learned. They were polished. But what this did to their hearts is demonstrated in the way they saw themselves and others—as "fair-I-see," standing above the crowd. They were proud of the fact that others did not in appearance live up to the standards of their own list of concerns.

Tragically, some churches today are full of legalists. These people define faith by a set of external rules and requirements. For legalists, faith is a list of "do this" and "don't do that." And in the midst of this system of self-imposed standardization, they lose the forest of grace in the trees of their own planting.

The second ditch is *liberalism*. The Sadducees best represent this in the New Testament. Since they didn't believe in the resurrection, they had no hope. It has been said that they were "sad-you-see." They did not take the truth of God seriously, and they failed to apply truth in life. To these people, faith was a license for exploration. Faith was what mattered, not substance or evidence. Faith was a venture to itself. And while the life of faith is indeed a great adventure, biblical faith is grounded in life and daily practice.

I have found that both of these ditches keep people from experiencing the freedom found in Jesus Christ.

Many issues become battleground issues for debate and conflict among believers. But here is the principle we must always remember: we are free in Christ, but our liberty is not the license to do anything and everything we want to do. "For you, brethren, have been called to liberty; only do not use liberty as an opportunity for the flesh, but through love serve one another. For all the law is fulfilled in one word . . . 'love your neighbor as yourself'" (Gal. 5:13–14).

We are to love others and care for their well-being. This is the first application of the principle of spiritual freedom. We have liberty in Jesus Christ, but our freedom does not propel us toward anything and everything we want.

So we proceed with Paul in his thinking on freedom in Christ.

The Principle of Individual Accountability

"Each of us shall give account of himself to God" (Rom. 14:12).

We have freedom in Christ, but with that freedom comes the understanding that we must always answer to the Lord. This is not to espouse *I'm OK, you're OK. Believe what you want, and I'll believe what I want.* Yes, we have been set free in Christ, but now we live our lives to honor Christ and to be accountable to Him.

Our job is not to judge others as it relates to some of the issues discussed in this chapter. Obviously, if someone, for example, is living his or her life in impurity, then that person comes under the authority of Scripture and the church. But as it relates to preferences—diet, days, practices, rituals—we are not to force others to conform to our preferred list of demands. Instead, we are to understand that the person to whom we must answer before God is ourselves. Someone once joked, "Faults in others I can see, but praise the Lord, there are none in me!"

> In other words, Christians are to live all of life as a stewardship to God.

In this passage, Paul makes a powerful point for us concerning lifestyle and behavior. He says, "For none of us lives to himself, and no one dies to himself. For if we live, we live to the Lord; and if we die, we die to the Lord. Therefore, whether we live or die, we are the Lord's" (Rom. 14:7–8).

In other words, Christians are to live all of life—top to bottom, day in and day out, morning and night—as a stewardship to God. We are His.

The Principle of Relational Responsibility

I heard about a man who had been married for fifty years. During the anniversary party, someone asked him to tell the group about the benefits of being married for so many years.

"Well," he said, "I've learned a lot of things over these fifty years. I've learned that marriage is the best teacher. It teaches you loyalty, meekness, forbearance, forgiveness, self-restraint, and a great many other qualities that you wouldn't need if you'd just stayed single."

We do not live unto ourselves. We live with and we live for the well-being of others.

The apostle Paul makes it clear that we have a responsibility not to knowingly and willingly cause a brother or sister to stumble. Peter also understood and affirmed this truth. He urged believers to "Act as free men, and do not use your freedom as a covering for evil, but use it as bondslaves of God" (1 Pet. 2:16 NASB).

Christians are slaves to the law of love. Therefore, when there is conflict, we should do everything we can to try to benefit our fellow brothers and sisters in Christ.

In Romans 14, Paul talks about those who are "weak"—those who eat only vegetables and who abstain from eating meat. Paul communicates that in a spirit of love, these believers should not be made to feel inferior. They should be received in a spirit of love. Conflict always comes when people assume spiritual superiority over others. Freedom comes when love and care are given to one another.

When a small child is in the home, the parents are happy to make adjustments to keep the child from injury. Furniture is padded or covered, breakables are placed higher on the shelves, trinkets are stored and locked, scissors are hidden, and sometimes safety gates are strategically placed around the home to keep the child from danger. No one thinks about the hassles or inconveniences of these changes because the child is loved and cherished. What is best for the child is best for the family.

This is the very principle Jesus addressed when He said, "Whoever causes one of these little ones who believe in Me to sin, it would be better for him if a millstone were hung around his neck, and he were drowned in the depth of the sea. Woe to the world because of offenses! For offenses must come, but woe to that man by whom the offense comes!" (Matt. 18:6–7).

As believers walking with Christ, we should do everything we can to help and encourage others to mature in their walk with Christ. We have a responsibility to remove the stumbling blocks.

These Principles in Action

Our discussion so far in this chapter has been general, but we all know there are specific issues that cause struggle, tension, and frustration among believers. So why not jump right in? Let's take a "for instance." My example may not be popular, but my point will be made. (By the way, one of the great leadership principles I have learned along the way in my life is that I cannot make everybody happy. I can, on the other hand, make everyone mad! So this won't be a first.)

> As believers walking with Christ, we should do everything we can to help and encourage others to mature in their walk with Christ.

What about the use of alcohol among believers? There's not much room for debate on the subject of alcohol abuse; alcoholism is an issue of consensus concern and challenge in our culture. You don't have to be a believer to find discussion and conviction on this subject. Just ask Mothers Against Drunk Driving (MADD). God bless their cause!

But what about social drinking? What about levels of alcoholic beverage use, beer and wine versus hard liquor, and cocktails among believers and as part of our fellowship together?

Why bother with this ongoing debate? Because I have great concern over a resurgence of issues related to our freedom in Christ among believers—young believers today, in particular—that may have lasting impact on our families, churches, and communities.

I am a Southern Baptist. And many of you know what they say about Baptists: "We don't drink, smoke, cuss, or chew—or go out with girls who do." But what I apply and practice on this matter has little to do with my denomination. I have no desire to be a Baptist Pharisee. But I do have a stewardship as a follower of Christ, and Paul's argument and challenge in Romans 14 presses the matter of my faith and practice to the outer limits of life in today's culture.

As a result of Paul's challenge to live responsibly, I choose to abstain from the use of alcohol in any form, except for the occasional dose of Nyquil for medicinal purposes. (I use Nyquil only as a last resort. I just hate that foggy feeling I have the morning after!)

In addition to my personal practice on this matter, I believe I can make a biblical case for extremely limited, if not restricted, use of alcohol. But whether you agree or argue with me concerning the presence and use of alcohol in Scripture, the issue of the presence and use of alcohol in our culture is of utmost importance in our lives, our relationships, and our witness to others.

Independence is a core value in America. Independence makes up the constitution of our lives in a free society. But Scripture binds us to a higher value and a greater practice, and that is relational responsibility. Ours is a way of life that refuses to indulge liberty at the expense of our responsibility to influence and encourage others.

As a believer, how can we take the most volatile, explosive, and damaging issue of our day—teenage experimentation and indulgence with alcohol—and think that what we say and do doesn't matter?

Numerous studies point to the fact that alcohol is the gateway drug of choice. Alcohol is the precedent to sexual indulgence, crime, use of illegal drugs, and many other irresponsible behaviors of all kinds. Some studies indicate that as many as one in four people who start to drink become alcoholics. I really struggle with saying, "Well,

I'm free in Christ, so I just do what I want to do." My liberty is a responsibility. I, for one, cannot downgrade for the sake of liberty what is at the core of so much upheaval in families, communities, and culture.

Study after study, case after case, and courtroom after courtroom present evidence time and time again that consumption and use of alcoholic beverages is a common denominator in the pain and destruction of human lives.

Just ask Oscar-winning actor and producer Mel Gibson. I will always be indebted to Mr. Gibson for the most vivid and telling portrait I've seen or experienced to date in his powerful portrayal of *The Passion of the Christ*. Yet the same man who delivered the message of the gospel with such compelling effectiveness later endured anger and ridicule because of offensive comments he made after being caught driving under the influence of alcohol.

As I watched the shame and scorn Mr. Gibson brought on himself, his family, and his reputation, I understood again why Solomon, the wise man, wrote: "Wine is a mocker, / Strong drink is a brawler, / And whoever is led astray by it is not wise" (Prov. 20:1). And then he later adds:

> Who has woe? Who has sorrow? Who has contentions? Who has complaints? Who has wounds without cause? Who has redness of eyes? Those who linger long at the wine, those who go in search of mixed wine. Do not look on the wine when it is red, when it sparkles in the cup, when it swirls around smoothly; at the last it bites like a serpent, and stings like a viper. Your eyes will see strange things, and your heart will utter perverse things. Yes, you will be like one who lies down in the midst of the sea, or like one who lies at the top of the mast, saying: "They have struck me, but I was not hurt; they have beaten me, but I did not feel it. When shall I awake, that I may seek another drink?" (Prov. 23:29–35)

Let me clearly state that my practice of abstaining from alcohol does not make me a better believer than others. But as a believer, I must live by a higher standard.

In my opinion, alcohol is the "meat" issue of our day. I cannot avoid, deny, or dismiss it. No, it is not the *summa sermonia* topic of my life, but when I think stewardship and freedom, I cannot help but be pushed to the edge of thought and practice on this subject. What I say in this area I do because of my relational responsibility and walk with Christ day by day.

Have you taken time to prayerfully consider your relational responsibility regarding this issue and others like it?

The Principle of Personal Testimony

As Christians, our personal testimony has to do with how we represent Christ to the world. As Paul says, "Therefore do not let your good be spoken of as evil; for the kingdom of God is not eating and drinking, but righteousness and peace and joy in the Holy Spirit. For he who serves Christ in these things is acceptable to God and approved by men. Therefore let us pursue the things which make for peace and the things by which one may edify another. Do not destroy the work of God for the sake of food. All things indeed are pure, but it is evil for the man who eats with offense" (Rom. 14:16–20).

> We sacrifice our life that we may give witness and testimony to the sacrifice of Christ.

It would be a terrible crime if someone entered a major art gallery with a spray can, aimed the spray at a masterpiece, and defaced a Monet, Rembrandt, or Da Vinci. How much worse is it when a Christian does something that defames the name of Jesus?

What we say, what we do, where we go, and all we are is about this new role and relationship called "living sacrifice" (Rom. 12:1). We sacrifice our life that we may give witness and testimony to the sacrifice of Christ.

This is more than my own interpretation and application of this text. Jesus gave this specific instruction to His followers: "Let your light so shine before men, that they may see your good works and glorify your Father in heaven" (Matt. 5:16).

We are free in Christ. As the Bible declares, "If the Son makes you free, you shall be free indeed" (John 8:36). But we are not to let our freedom become a license for indulgence or irresponsibility. Instead, we should let our freedom in Christ be the standard by which we lift ourselves and other believers to live lovingly, graciously, and responsibly to the glory of Jesus Christ.

chapter 15

we are liberated to live responsibly

The passion of Christianity is that I deliberately sign away my own rights and become a bond-slave of Jesus Christ. Until I do that, I do not begin to be a saint.

—Oswald Chambers[2]

"For none of us lives to himself, and no one dies to himself. For if we live, we live to the Lord; and if we die, we die to the Lord. Therefore, whether we live or die, we are the Lord's. For to this end Christ died and rose and lived again, that He might be Lord of both the dead and the living. . . . So then each of us shall give account of himself to God" (Rom. 14:7–9, 12).

We have been liberated in Christ, and we are to use that liberty responsibly.

The Principle of Spiritual Liberty

"There is therefore now no condemnation to those who are in Christ Jesus, who do not walk according to the flesh, but according to the Spirit. For the law of the Spirit of life in Christ Jesus has made me free from the law of sin and death" (Rom. 8:1–2).

But remember, liberty is not the license to do anything and everything we want to do.

"For you, brethren, have been called to liberty; only do not use liberty as an opportunity for the flesh, but through love serve one another. For all the law is fulfilled in one word . . . 'love your neighbor as yourself' " (Gal. 5:13–14).

The Principle of Individual Accountability

"So then each of us shall give account of himself to God" (Rom. 14:12).

The Principle of Relational Responsibility

"Whoever causes one of these little ones who believe in Me to sin, it would be better for him if a millstone were hung around his neck, and he were drowned in the depth of the sea. Woe to the world because of offenses! For offenses must come, but woe to that man by whom the offense comes!" (Matt. 18:6–7).

The Principle of Personal Testimony

Your personal testimony has to do with how you represent Christ to the world. It would be a terrible crime if someone entered a major art gallery with a spray can, aimed the spray at a masterpiece, and defaced a Monet, Rembrant, or DaVinci of the world. How much worse is it when a Christian does something that defames the name of Jesus?

"Let your light so shine before men, that they may see your good works and glorify your Father in heaven" (Matt. 5:16).

we are strengthened to encourage

Recently I read about a secret weapon used during World War II. What I discovered exposed my ignorance and captured my attention. Although I was a history major in college, I have to admit I'd never heard of the strategic use of this weapon of mass distribution.

On the campus of colleges and universities, a handful of history buffs debate the turning points of war and peace in our world, pointing to time lines, military strategies, sociopolitical issues, and the development of refined weaponry. But I was amazed to learn the strategic role and significant contribution made by a rather common item—the prune.

That's right, the prune. Not long ago, a London auction house sold two dried prunes that had been prepared and preserved as strategic weapons from World War II. How? Apparently prunes were softened in water, pitted, dried, and subsequently stuffed with wax paper. Then maps or other forms of strategic intelligence were placed in them and sent to prisoners of war. They were also given to the wounded and injured in Red Cross facilities during wartime.

The result was a small, unassuming, yet strategic weapon that provided a network for communication that facilitated direction, sabotage, and other vital information for troops and commanders alike.

Isn't it amazing to consider that prunes provided strength and encouragement for needy soldiers? Of course, it wasn't the prune per se but what the prune provided that made all the difference in the lives of Allied troops—hope.

Hope Is Vital

Hope is vital for life. It may be no more than a prune in a prison cell or a hospital bed, but hope feeds faith and fuels our determination to carry on. Hope gives breath to the weary and light to those who fear the shadows of darkness.

For this reason, the apostle Paul prayed and penned these words to the hearts of first-century Christ followers in Rome: "Now may the God of hope fill you with all joy and peace in believing, that you may abound in hope by the power of the Holy Spirit" (Rom. 15:13).

> Hope is vital for life.

In Romans 15, Paul makes it clear that we need hope. The strength we receive in hope enables us to encourage others and build them up in faith.

We are strengthened to encourage. And we encourage one another through mutual acceptance and support by the grace and mercy God has measured out and into our lives. We do not live to please ourselves or to focus on our individual survival instincts but rather to bear with and help others bear up under the burdens and struggles of life. This includes those weak in the faith and those who are weary on the road of life.

Eugene Petersen does a masterful job giving expression to the emphasis of the opening words of Romans 15. He challenges us to an understanding that what God has done and is doing in our lives is to bring us into a harmony of hope with other believers. Take a moment to read and reflect on these words:

> Those of us who are strong and able in the faith need to step in and lend a hand to those who falter, and not just do what is most convenient for us. Strength is for service, not status. Each one of us needs to look after the good of the people around us, asking ourselves, "How can I help?" That's exactly what Jesus

did. He didn't make it easy for himself by avoiding people's troubles, but waded right in and helped out. "I took on the troubles of the troubled," is the way Scripture puts it. Even if it was written in Scripture long ago, you can be sure it's written for us. God wants the combination of his steady, constant calling and warm, personal counsel in Scripture to come to characterize us, keeping us alert for whatever he will do next. May our dependably steady and warmly personal God develop maturity in you so that you get along with each other as well as Jesus gets along with us all. Then we'll be a choir—not our voices only, but our very lives singing in harmony in a stunning anthem to the God and Father of our Master Jesus! (Rom. 15:1–6 MSG)

God wants us to know and to share common hope. In Christ, we are never beyond and never without hope.

Hope Is to Be Shared with Others

The grace and mercy we receive in moments of need, challenge, and pain are the very things God wants to use in the lives of others in their hour of need.

> The grace and mercy we receive in moments of need, challenge, and pain are the very things God wants to use in the lives of others in their hour of need.

It has been God's plan through the ages to teach truth through the life experiences of others. It is the stewardship of hardship. When we read words like Romans 15:4—"For whatever things were written before were written for our learning, that we through the patience and comfort of the Scriptures might have hope"—we begin to understand that God touches and encourages us through the grace and strength He provided through others who have gone before us.

God's movement in time, space, and history; His works seen in human personality, weakness, and pain; and His grace measured in prophecy and promise all point toward a source of strength and encouragement in life's hour of need—the Scriptures. God's Word is truth for life.

Many people who have gone before us had experiences in life that were recorded in the pages of Scripture. These experiences included faith, failure, and difficulty. Their stories were given to us by the power of the Holy Spirit so that their struggles might encourage us in our struggles, their fears might help us when we fear, and their faith might boost our faith when we feel that we are facing impossible odds. This record—the Bible— was written for our learning or for instructional information. That means it is functional for use in daily life. It is a reminder of the providence of God and the processes by which He works in our lives.

> We all need the encouragement of God's truth to help us focus, persevere, and move ahead.

Even when we see nations rising and crisis coming on the horizons of history, the plan and the purpose of God are still fulfilled. Whether we look at the masterful view of history and the rise and fall of civilization or whether we look at the biographies of men and women of faith who have walked with God, all of this was written in Scripture to give us perspective and remind us that God is working today and to encourage us.

Not only does the Word of God give us a picture of God's work in days gone by, but it fills our hearts with promise of what God will do for us as we seek Him, as we trust Him, and as we lean upon Him.

We all need the encouragement of God's truth to help us focus, persevere, and move ahead. Yet His truth is more than formal tutorial. There are absolute precepts and fundamental principles, but in God's wisdom and grace, He presents truth and proves His truth in our lives as we make the journey by faith.

The Bible is much more than a formal, complex manual. It is a living book, dynamic and strategic, providing framework for both ethic and experience. It is unrivaled in relevance, unchanging in truth, and unwavering in authority. Wherever we are and whatever we face, God's Word provides God's perspective and promise for life.

Having said that, God's Word captures scenes of experience and stories that provide instruction and encouragement for us all. As we follow the footsteps of others who have journeyed by faith, we grow in our own faith and in grace to share with others facing life's challenges with us today.

> All of us need strength and encouragement.

The tone of Romans 15 is that of striving, struggling, and strengthening one another. It is no wonder that Paul closes the chapter with these words: ". . . that I may come to you with joy by the will of God, and may be refreshed together with you. Now the God of peace be with you all. Amen" (vv. 32–33).

Hope Can Overcome Discouragement

All of us need strength and encouragement. As it has been said, "It is a rare person who does not get discouraged." During times of discouragement, God's provision for us—the strength we receive through hope—becomes the very source by which we encourage others along life's road.

Are you discouraged today? Discouragement is such a common experience for us all. Discouragement comes from many sources: failed dreams, frustrated expectations, an unfulfilled promise, unjust criticism, fatigue, or a setback. While the sources may vary and the circumstances may change by degree, discouragement relates to our struggle to reckon with God's grace in the place we find ourselves in life.

Are you facing criticism?

Are you dealing with failure?

Are you struggling with pain?

Are you battling an illness?

Are you wrestling with disappointment?

Are you hurting because someone let you down?

Are you dealing with loss?

Are you being harassed by Satan?

All these and more push us to the place of discouragement. And discouragement causes us to doubt God. In fact, in many ways, discouragement is wrestling with and even refusing to accept God's plan and work in our lives.

We often think because we hurt, God must be absent. Yet Paul teaches just the opposite: God works in and through our pain. "Now may the God of hope fill you with all joy and peace *in believing*, that you may abound in hope by the power of the Holy Spirit" (Rom. 15:13; emphasis added).

> We are strengthened that we may encourage others also.

One such place of hope and perspective on hardship was offered earlier in Romans 8:28: "We know that all things work together for good to those who love God, to those who are the called according to His purpose." Can I call Him Lord and not trust His presence, plan, and promise in my pain?

Paul knew that the believers in Rome faced resistance, endured hardship, and needed encouragement. For this reason he wanted to be with them and to minister to them the strength he had received through his own struggles.

And it is for this same reason we are strengthened that we may encourage others also.

Hope and Strength for Today

Before I close this chapter, let me offer four words that may provide added hope and strength for us all today.

Review

Look back and remember how God worked and moved in the lives of those who have gone before us. For them, life was not painless; instead, faith was often painstaking. Joseph was criticized, mistreated, and falsely accused on his way to the pinnacle of leadership in Egypt. Moses was frustrated by the pace and progress of his effort to fulfill God's plan. Hosea had a heart for God and a wife whose body belonged to everyone else but his own. And even our Lord Jesus Christ "learned obedience by the things which He suffered" (Heb. 5:8).

While the works and ways of God are a mystery, there is consistent testimony and a firm promise that "whatever things were written before were written for our learning, that we through the patience and comfort of the Scriptures might have hope" (Rom. 15:4).

Reclaim

Because of what Christ has done for us, we can affirm and reclaim God's promise to work in our lives also. While His plans and purposes may change, God's power is not limited, and His promise is not void or embraced in vain.

Throughout the fifteenth chapter of Romans, Paul talks about his calling to preach to the Gentiles and about God's offer of mercy and grace to those who were not Jews. He talks of his travels, his struggles, and their prayers on his behalf. Yet in the midst of all such strife, he speaks of joy and peace.

This same joy and peace can be yours and mine by God's promise. When life holds us down, keeps us back, and threatens to take us under, God's promise will see us through. Maybe we need to pause and reclaim God's promise of grace, mercy, and strength to help us in our hour of need.

Refresh

Stress, strain, and struggle all wear on the mind and body. Paul knew weariness. But he spoke of a day when he would join with fellow believers in Rome and, together, they would be "refreshed" (Rom. 15:32).

God often uses faith-building relationships to refresh our weary hearts. One of the things the enemy, Satan, likes to do is to get us isolated and separated from fellowship with other believers. The more alone we feel, the less allegiance we will have to the purpose of God in our lives. We need the strength and encouragement of other believers. They cannot remove our pains, but they can and do help bear our burdens.

My friend Wes once sent me a short poem his grandfather used to share with him. These words express the added value of friendship and refreshment:

> It is my joy in life to find
> At every turning of the road
> The strong arm of a comrade kind
> To help me onward with my load
> And since I have not gold to give;
> And love itself must make amends
> My constant prayer is while I live
> God make me worthy of my friends.[1]

Pay attention to the condition of your mind, your body, and your friends. All of these can help you be refreshed and enable you to refresh others also.

Refocus

It's easy to lose focus and face discouragement. I was reminded of this again recently when I read of an eighty-two-year-old woman who received a $114 ticket for taking too long to get across the street in San Fernando Valley, California. She was cited as being an obstruction to traffic because she was unable to get to the other side of the street at the intersection before the light changed. To his defense, the spokesman for the LA police said, "I would rather not have angry pedestrians, but I'd rather have them alive."[2] True.

Obviously, someone instructed officers on the beat to crack down on slow pedestrians. But a $114 ticket? I would say that would discourage anyone from crossing any streets in LA by foot. I'm sure there's at least one little old lady pedestrian who doesn't have much courage or confidence when it comes to walking across the street.

> If God exists—and He does—then our focus on God changes everything.

If you pause in the intersection of life to consider what discourages you, you will find it is those moments and events that undermine your confidence and diminish your courage. Who can forget the heartless lion in the *Wizard of Oz*? He was weak and anxious because he lacked courage. What should have been the signature in his soul had become the point of his disgrace.

So it is with us as believers. Faith is the signature of the Christian life, but when fear and anxiety overwhelm us, we lose our focus and confidence in God. Note the repetition from Paul's pen: "Now may the God of patience and comfort grant you to be like-minded toward one another," (Rom. 15:5) and then again, "Now the God of peace" (Rom. 15:33). Here and many other times, Paul makes God the point of reference in his own strength and in affirming strength for the believers in Rome.

God Is the Source of Hope

In many ways, it all comes down to this: either there is a God we can know, believe, and trust—or there is no god at all. Without God, we have no hope. Life is simply a tragic existence with limited control and uncertain outcome. But if God exists—and *He does*—then our focus on God changes everything.

In Romans 15, Paul speaks of "the God of patience and comfort," "the God of mercy," "the God of hope," "the grace of God," "the gospel of God," "the will of God," and "the God of peace." A God-focused life is the key to confidence, courage, and comfort.

So take a moment—right now—to pause and seek renewed strength in your life. Remember the words of the prophet Isaiah:

> Have you not known? Have you not heard? The everlasting God, the Lord, the Creator of the ends of the earth, neither faints nor is weary. His understanding is unsearchable. He gives power to the weak, and *to* those who have no might He increases strength. Even the youths shall faint and be weary, and the young men shall utterly fall, but those who wait on the Lord shall renew their strength; they shall mount up with wings like eagles, they shall run and not be weary, and they shall walk and not faint. (Isa. 40:28–31)

God wants to renew your strength, but not just for you alone. For when your strength is renewed, then you are able to encourage others who are weary, worn, and needy. God desires that we become "stewards" of the hardships in our life, so that we can use our experience to provide help and hope for others in need.

And so I echo Paul's prayer for you today: "Now the God of peace be with you all. Amen" (Rom. 15:33).

we are strengthened to encourage

This is the true joy in life, the being used for a purpose recognized by yourself as a mighty one; the being thoroughly worn out before you are thrown on the scrap heap; the being a force of nature instead of a feverish selfish little clod of ailments, and grievances complaining that the world will not devote itself to making you happy.

—George Bernard Shaw[3]

Hope Is Vital

"Those of us who are strong and able in the faith need to step in and lend a hand to those who falter, and not just do what is most convenient for us. Strength is for service, not status. Each one of us needs to look after the good of the people around us, asking ourselves, 'How can I help?'" (Rom. 15:1–2 MSG).

Hope Is to Be Shared with Others

The grace and mercy we receive in moments of need, challenge, and pain are the very things God wants to use in the lives of others in their hour of need.

God's movement in time, space, and history; His works seen in human personality, weakness, and pain; and His grace measured in prophecy and promise all point toward a source of strength and encouragement in life's hour of need: the Scriptures.

Hope Can Overcome Discouragement

Discouragement is our struggle to reckon with God's grace in the place we find ourselves in life.

Hope and Strength for Today

"Now may the God of hope fill you with all joy and peace in believing, that you may abound in hope by the power of the Holy Spirit" (Rom. 15:13).

• *Review*. Look back and remember how God worked and moved in the lives of those who have gone before us.

• *Reclaim*. Because of what Christ has done for us, we can affirm and reclaim God's promise to work in our lives also. God knows how to get you out of trouble; He hasn't forgotten how to part the sea.

• *Refresh*. Stress, strain, and struggle all wear on the mind and body.

• *Refocus*. It's easy to lose focus and face discouragement.

"Have you not known? Have you not heard? The everlasting God, the LORD, the Creator of the ends of the earth, neither faints nor is weary . . . . He gives power to the weak, and to those who have no might He increases strength." (Isa. 40:28–29).

You are strengthened to encourage. There is a stewardship of hardship in your life that provides help and hope for others in need.

"Now the God of peace be with you all. Amen" (Rom. 15:33).

chapter 17
we are blessed to be a blessing

For everyone to whom much is given,
from him much will be required.
—LUKE 12:48

Everything we have, we have been given.

We've come full circle. From the beginning, these words helped shape the thought and direction of this book. This is the perspective from which I have written as I have journeyed in my own life and faith to discover what it is to be faithful in the stewardship of my life and walk with Christ.

As Paul closes the magnificent book of Romans, he does so with personal reflection and appeal. I find it fascinating that a book so weighted with doctrine and instruction closes with an extended list of names of people who have encouraged and supported Paul in the work to which he was called.

Gratitude Is a Sign of Greatness

As Paul closes his letter to the church in Rome, he says, "I commend to you Phoebe our sister . . ." (Rom. 16:1). With these words, he launches a list of greetings, endorsements, and thanks.

Paul understood that he was blessed by others and that his life, like theirs, was intended to be a source of blessing to others also. We are blessed to be a blessing.

If it is true that everything we have, we have been given, then in everything we give, we share the blessing of a life of investment and encouragement through those who have loved and helped us.

> We are blessed to be a blessing.

When we look at life from God's perspective, we quickly observe that we are much more debtors than we are achievers in life. So much of what we consider ours is really nothing more than the cumulative impact of God's mercy and grace and the influence of others He has placed in the pathway of our life.

I've observed through the years that a true sign of greatness is gratitude. When truly great people excel at, accomplish, or achieve something, they are quick to point to others who have sacrificed and invested in them along the way.

They don't take the credit who share the glory and the praise.

A Debtor to a Father's Love

Tiger Woods is known as a fierce competitor. His presence intimidates fellow competitors in any golf tournament, since everyone knows that Tiger can "own" Sundays in the final round.

But recently, the world got a glimpse of a "tamer Tiger." We saw the softer side of this young man's heart in the days following the death of his father, mentor, and enduring coach, Earl Woods.

Speaking of his father and their relationship, Tiger said, "He is the person I looked up to more than any other." In an interview in *Golf Digest* in 2001, Earl Woods said, "My purpose in raising Tiger was not to raise a golfer. I wanted to raise a good person."[1]

From start to finish, this was Earl's goal. Tiger's achievements, accolades, accomplishments, and awards—these did not come because of rehearsal or regimen; rather, they were all by-products of a relationship between a father and a son.

I love the words of Eugene Robinson in his *Washington Post* article following Earl's death: "I found myself unexpectedly moved by the death of Earl Woods, who succumbed to prostate cancer . . . since I never met the man. I knew him only through what the public has been able to see of his relationship with his son, Tiger. . . . Eventually, I realize the reason I feel such a sense of loss is that I'll never get to witness that remarkable relationship again."[2] Earl Woods was a father whose presence made all the difference in a world where the absence of fathers is felt every day.

In the end, Tiger said of his dad, "My dad was my best friend and greatest role model, and I will miss him deeply. I wouldn't be where I am today without him."[3]

While Tiger is certainly a great winner, he is also a debtor to the life and legacy of a dad who invested much in him.

Thank-You Notes for Your Life

When you think about it, there are many thank-you notes you could send if you take time to look back through the rearview mirror of life. Some are long past, while others continue today.

I'll list a few of mine.

My grandparents, Ken and Eunice McKinley, hosted us for holidays, took me fishing, and provided support when I attended seminary. Also, my maternal grandparents, Joseph and Rose Jeanette Mason.

> There are many thank-you notes you could send if you take time to look back through the rearview mirror of life.

Grandfather Joseph was a pastor, and I have his Bible in my library today. He died shortly after I was born, but I spent many wonderful and memorable summers with my Grandmother Jan as a child. We caught fireflies in a bottle, made raisin toast in the mornings, and counted cars on the porch in the evenings.

My parents, Harold and Jeanne, marked fifty years together. They loved, cared for, nurtured, and made provisions for me. I am indebted to them for their sacrifice, devotion, and investment in me. My parents, along with my brother Rick, provided a steady, happy, and secure home life. I am deeply grateful for my family. Rick is six years my younger. He is one of the finest Christian men I know, and I am incredibly proud of his leadership in the world of business and his faithfulness as a follower of Christ.

Many family friends hosted us, traveled with us, and took us to the lake for Sunday afternoons swimming, eating fried chicken, and churning ice cream as a kid.

As a child, I had many Sunday school teachers who prepared, taught, and faithfully invested in my life to help me learn the Bible. In particular, I am grateful to Ruth Gamble, a Bible teacher who challenged me as a minimally–motivated high school student to excel and apply myself with diligence to get a grasp of God's Word.

Pastor Wayne Allen pulled me aside at age sixteen and said, "I want you to preach in chapel." So I preached my first sermon on May 5, 1977, to more than one thousand students at my high school. I still remember the fear and weakness I felt as I walked to the podium quoting, "I can do all things through Christ who strengthens me" (Phil. 4:13).

Ken Whitten and other campus ministers at my church helped to disciple me. They challenged and instructed me to help me walk with Christ each day.

It was in those days, in college, when I met Connie, God's life gift to me. Connie is my bride, and though I accidentally dropped her while trying to be a showoff at our wedding rehearsal, she married me anyway. Although that was not the last time I "let her down," she has believed in me and walked with me through these past twenty-eight years. Connie is bright, beautiful, and hardworking. There were many things she could have done for herself, but she has sacrificed to share life with me. Since she made a commitment to "do life" with me in 1979, she has supported me in ministry, loved me through difficulty, prepared some of the best meals and desserts I have ever eaten this side of heaven, attended to our home and family, and makes the journey of life richer and sweeter every day through her love, faithfulness, forgiveness, and desire to complete me in every way. All I can say is that Solomon was exactly right when he said, "He who finds a wife finds a good thing, / And obtains the favor from the LORD" (Prov. 18:22).

Dr. B. Gray Allison, the founder and president of Mid-America Seminary, where I attended, imprinted my life with his passion for a lost world and the essential need for every believer to be a daily witness for Christ. To this day when I think of him, I think of Acts 20:20–21 and the need to never "hold back" in sharing my faith.

R. C. Henderson, my Greek professor and an incredible man, had a passion for Scripture that challenged my discipline and shaped my habits in study. Dr. Henderson was educated at the University of Edinburgh and spent more than a decade as a missionary in Africa. I loved him and built a relationship with him I intended to enjoy across a lifetime of ministry, but he died suddenly and unexpectedly in his early fifties, five days after my graduation from seminary.

Friends, too many for me to name, whose faces quickly surface in my mind, remind me of God's grace in my life. They have encouraged me, supported me, challenged me, comforted me, prayed for me, and blessed me. I can only imagine those in Rome who read Paul's letter and smiled because they were included in his closing remarks. I also wonder if there are those who read the letter and thought, *Hey, he didn't mention me!* Since these words do not bear the marks of divine inspiration, I will simply say, "Thank you, friends—you know who you are!"

My pastors R. G. Lee and Ramsey Pollard influenced me as a child and in the early years of my spiritual formation. These men were stalwart leaders and voices of their generation. But it was Adrian Rogers and Jack Graham who imprinted my life through their voices, leadership, and love. While each of these men made distinct and unique contributions to my faith, development, and Christian service, it was Dr. Rogers who had a "reality relationship" with Christ and a voice of truth that captured my heart and compelled me to follow Christ. It was Jack Graham who saw potential in me as a seminary graduate and gave me the opportunity, experience, and a lifetime of friendship that continues to bless my life today. Jack and his wife, Deb, are two of the finest, greatest, and best people I know.

I am also grateful to the churches who loved and encouraged me: my "home church," Bellevue Baptist Church in Memphis, Tennessee; my "first" church, First Baptist Church in West Palm Beach, Florida; and then the joy of serving as pastor in Merritt Island and Boca Raton, Florida. Each fellowship has been filled with people, projects, and experiences that have made all the difference in my life and my family.

> The life we are born to live is the life we are born to give.

And then there is Prestonwood—a double blessing. It was an experience so good, it was worth repeating by God's grace. These places and the people we have known and loved have put praise in my heart beyond words. Together, we shared a passion to proclaim the gospel of Jesus Christ. And this passion, coupled with these churches' positive encouragement and personal sacrifice, have allowed Connie and me in different places, at different times, and in different seasons to live lives of purpose for the Lord Jesus Christ.

An assortment of mentors including Billy Graham, Bill Bright, George Sweeting, Joe Stowell, John McArthur, Chuck Swindoll, Warren Weirsbe, Jerry Vines, D. James Kennedy, Tony Evans, John Maxwell, Rick Warren, Zig Ziglar, and so many more have made a lasting mark on my life. Most have influenced me from a distance. Several I have had the privilege of calling friends.

And then, I can't make such a list and not make mention of my two fantastic kids, Joseph and Mary Elizabeth. Theirs is a story in itself. After seven years of marriage and the difficult realization we could not have children naturally, Connie and I discovered that God provided something better for us: He gave us our children. Through the life journey we have shared with Joe and Lizzi, we have come to understand that God sometimes allows us to travel pathways we wouldn't have initially chosen to experience the blessings we could never have otherwise comprehended.

I haven't scratched the surface. But you get the picture:

What we have, we have been given.

We are blessed to be a blessing.

That's what Paul was saying, doing, and sharing as he closed the book. He was blessed to be a blessing, and his life and ministry were blessed by others who knew and did the same.

The life we are born to live is the life we are born to give.

My life—your life—is not our own. As believers, we are bought with a price and live to give glory to God and be a blessing to others as we make this journey. So however long we live, may we never forget or lose sight of this truth:

The life you were born to live is the life you were born to give.

we are blessed to be a blessing

*There is a destiny that makes us brothers; no one goes alone. All that
we send into the lives of others comes back into our own.*

—*Jeffrey Marx*

Everything we have, we have been given.

Gratitude Is a Sign of Greatness

As Paul closes the magnificent book of Romans, he does so with personal reflection and appeal. I find it fascinating that a book so weighed with doctrine and instruction would close with an extended list of names of people who have encouraged and supported Paul in the work to which he was called. He closes with endearing words of appreciation and affection.

"I commend to you Phoebe our sister . . ." (Rom. 16:1). With these words, Paul launches a list of greetings, endorsements, and thanks.

Paul understood that he was blessed by others and that his life, like theirs, was intended to be a source of blessing to others also.

When we look at life from God's perspective, we quickly observe that we are much more debtors than we are achievers in life. So much of what we consider ours is really nothing more than the cumulative impact of God's mercy and grace and the influence of others He has placed in the pathway of our life.

Thank-You Notes for Your Life

There are many thank-you notes you could send if you take time to look back through the rearview mirror of life. Pause and make a mental list in order to offer thanks to God.

"O Lord, I know the way of man is not in himself; it is not in man who walks to direct his own steps" (Jer. 10:23).

The Life You Were Born to Give

Your life is not your own. As believers, we are bought with a price and live to give glory to God and be a blessing to others as we make this journey.

However long we live, we never want to forget or lose sight of this truth: the life we are born to live is the life we are born to give.

a personal or group study guide

Chapter 1: A Global System Failure

1. Take time to read Romans 1–3 and highlight key verses.
2. In what ways did the fall of Adam and Eve affect human behavior and culture?
3. How would you explain the phrase "fall short" in Romans 3:23?
4. Based on what you learn in Romans 3:9–18, how does God view us?
5. According to Romans 3:21–31, God desires a relationship with us based on what? How is this realized or achieved?

Chapter 2: The Ultimate Injustice

1. Read and reflect on Romans 5.
2. What does Romans 5:1 reveal about how we can have "peace with God"?
3. What do you observe about God's love in Romans 5:6–11?
4. What is significant about the contrast between Adam and Christ in Romans 5:15–17?
5. In what ways can the work of Christ be considered "the ultimate injustice"?

Chapter 3: Restart for New Life

1. What is the significance of Paul's question in Romans 6:1?
2. According to Romans 6:4, what is God's plan once a person receives Christ?

3. Romans 6:6, 11, 13 provide insights about our deliverance from the old dominance of sin and a call to a new life empowered by grace. What do you observe?
4. Based on what you have learned in Romans 6 and this book, describe the spiritual "upgrade" available for true believers.
5. What area(s) of your life do you need to yield to God? What specific steps will you take to do so?

Chapter 4: The Firewall of God's Love

1. Read Romans 8:31–39. Based on these verses, how would you describe the love of God to someone?
2. List the five essential questions presented in Romans 8:31–39.
3. How does God's enduring and unfailing love apply to your life and circumstances today?
4. Why is Romans 8:28 such an important truth for believers?
5. What do you think the apostle Paul is implying when he declares in Romans 8:37, "We are more than conquerors through Him who loved us?"

Chapter 5: Time to Rethink Everything

1. What are some causes of ineffectiveness in life?
2. Why are common signs of a "sponge" mentality or practice in your life or church?
3. Read Romans 11:33–36 and describe at least three insights from these verses.
4. What do you learn about stewardship from this chapter?
5. What does the phrase "a life delivered" mean?

Chapter 6: A Change of Heart

1. What is the context of the "therefore" in Romans 12:1?
2. Why is Romans 12:1–2 so important to the overall message of the book?

3. Write Romans 12:1–2 in your own words and personalize it. (Consider reading these verses in several translations.)
4. What is the significance of Paul's appeal to God's mercy in this passage?
5. Read and reflect on the words to "When I Survey the Wondrous Cross" on page 47.

Chapter 7: A Change of Mind

1. How does the world around us impact our thoughts?
2. Why are our thoughts the keys to spiritual transformation?
3. What do you learn about thoughts from 2 Corinthians 10:3–6?
4. What is the "mind of Christ" referenced in Philippians 2?
5. How does the quote by A. W. Tozer on page 52 relate to Romans 12:1–2?

Chapter 8: A Change of Will

1. What is the essential insight we learn about "God's will" on page 55? How does this apply to you?
2. Jim Elliot said, "When it comes time to die, make sure all you have to do is die" (see p. 55). What are your thoughts about this view of success?
3. How is God's will described in Romans 12:2, and what are the implications of each of these descriptions?
4. How does Romans 12:1–2 relate to the concept of holiness?
5. Much attention is given to "knowing God's will," but much less to "proving God's will." Is there an area of your life where you need to "prove God"?

Chapter 9: We Are Gifted to Serve

1. List the seven service gifts found in Romans 12:6–8.
2. Have you identified your primary spiritual gift? If so, what is it? If not, go to www.churchgrowth.org for a free profile.

3. What do you learn about spiritual gifts from Arthur T. Pierson's statement on page 74?

4. How does Romans 12:3 relate to Paul's instruction to "outsource" life in Romans 12:1–2?

5. What is the word picture used in Romans 12:4–5 to describe the mutual function of spiritual gifts?

Chapter 10: We Are Lifted to Love

1. What does the word *fellowship* mean, and why it is important to Christians today?

2. In what ways is love the foundational principle of all relationships?

3. Examine the Ten Commandments of Authentic Fellowship on pages 78–84, and identify two areas that require attention from you and from your church.

4. Read John 15:12–13. What is the highest demand of true love?

5. If you are a believer, why is your behavior so important?

Chapter 11: We Are Shaped by Experiences

1. What is the most common and natural of all human responses to hurt, loss, or injury?

2. What is the problem with payback, as described in this chapter?

3. How do the verses at the end of Romans 12 (vv. 17–21) relate to the verses at the beginning of the chapter (vv. 1–2)?

4. How do we sometimes "waste" our sorrow and struggles in life?

5. Instead of seeking payback when we are wronged, how can we be good stewards in life's hardships?

Chapter 12: We Are Called to Influence

1. List several applications of Romans 13:1–7 to your role as a citizen.

2. What does the Bible teach about authority in Romans 13?

3. In a day where the emphasis on "rights" seems to supersede "responsibilities," what must we observe in Romans 13 about citizenship?

4. How does the Bible describe the role of law enforcement in government, and how should we relate to those who serve in this way?

5. Why do you think Paul spent so much time in this passage on the subject of citizenship?

Chapter 13: We Are Entrusted to Invest

1. Review and reflect on 1 Timothy 6:9–10, and then list some observations about material possessions and financial gains.

2. How does God want us to view our money? (Review Matt. 6:19–21; 6:24; 2 Cor. 9:6–10; 1 Tim. 6:17–19.)

3. Read Romans 13:7 and Mark 12:16. How would you describe "fiscal responsibility" in the life of a Christian?

4. According to Romans 13:8, what is our greatest obligation in life? How does it relate to money?

5. What do you "owe" God?

Chapter 14: We Are Tested by Time

1. Read and reflect on Romans 13:11–14.

2. Why is time management important for every believer?

3. Take time to evaluate your clock and calendar over the past week. What do you observe?

4. How does the matter of time management discussed in this chapter relate to the call to be a living sacrifice in Romans 12:1–2?

5. List three things you need to make time for this week.

Chapter 15: We Are Liberated to Live Responsibly

1. How would you define *freedom* in the life of a Christian?

2. What does Romans 14 teach us about Christian liberties? Would you describe this passage as insights, warnings, or instructions?

3. What governs and protects our freedom in Christ? (Hint: read Romans 14:12, 19, 23.)

4. What are some issues of "liberty" you are facing today, and how do the principles described in this chapter relate to those situations?

5. According to Romans 14:13, how do our behavior choices affect other believers?

Chapter 16: We Are Strengthened to Encourage

1. Who is your favorite biblical character and why?

2. What do we learn about God from Old Testament witnesses?

3. What are some common causes of discouragement in your life?

4. How do the four words provided on pages 156–57 help you find strength for challenges you face today? How can you apply them?

5. What does Romans 15:5–6 tell us about God's work and desire in our life's difficulties?

Chapter 17: We Are Blessed to Be a Blessing

1. What are your thoughts about the opening sentences of chapter 1 and chapter 17 of this book?

2. Take time to list the names of and thank God for several key contributors in your life's journey.

3. Write an action plan for remembering and acknowledging those who have blessed your life.

4. How can you pass along the investments others have made in you?

5. Personalize this sentence: "The life I am born to live is . . ."

notes

Chapter 1—A Global System Failure

1. Max Lucado, "What Katrina Can Teach Us," sermon preached at Oak Hills Church, San Antonio, TX, 11 September 2005. Used by permission.
2. Al Mohler, "God in the Storm—Part Two," 8 September 2005, http://www.albertmohler.com/commentary. Used by permission.
3. H. L.Willmington, *Willmington's Guide to the Bible* (Wheaton, Ill.: Tyndale House Publishers, 1982), 446-47.
4. Ibid., 449.
5. Lucado, "What Katrina Can Teach Us."

Chapter 2—The Ultimate Injustice

1. John Gibson, "Moronic Judges," FOX News, 6 January 2006, http://www.foxnews.com/story/0,2933,180915,00.html
2. Interview with author, April 2006.

Chapter 3—Restart to a New Life

1. Paul Little, *Know What You Believe* (Colorado Springs: Chariot Victor, a division of Cook Communications, 2003),76 77. Used by permission. To order, www.cookministries.com. All rights reserved.
2. Taken from *The Saving Life of Christ* by Major Ian W. Thomas. Copyright © 1961 by Zondervan Publishing House. Used by permission of Zondervan.
3. Ibid., 13.

Chapter 5—Time to Rethink Everything

1. Chris Fabry, *The 77 Habits of Highly Ineffective Christians* (Downers Grove, IL: InterVarsity, 1997), dedication. Used by permission. Chrisfabry@adelphia.net.
2. Ibid., 22–23.
3. Colin Brown, *New International Dictionary of New Testament Theology* (Grand Rapids, MI: Zondervan, 1986), 247–58.
4. R. Leonard Carroll, *Stewardship: Total Life Commitment* (Cleveland, TN: Pathway, 1967), 32. Used by permission.

Chapter 6—A Change of Heart

1. Frank E. Gaebelein, *The Expositor's Bible Commentary*, Vol. 10 (Grand Rapids: Zondervan, 1992), 126.
2. Taken from *My Utmost for His Highest* by Oswald Chambers, © 1935 by Dodd Mead & Co., renewed © 1963 by the Oswald Chambers Publications Assn., Ltd. Used by permission of Discovery House Publishers, Grand Rapids, MI 49501. All rights reserved.

Chapter 7—A Change of Mind

1. Rick Warren, The Purpose-Driven Life (Grand Rapids, MI: Zondervan, 2002), 17.
2. Reprinted from *Man: The Dwelling Place of God* by A.W. Tozer, copyright © 1966 by Zur Ltd. Used by permission of WingSpread Publishers, a division of Zur Ltd., 800.884.4571.
3. W. Glyn Evans, *Daily with the King* (Chicago: Moody, 1989). Used by permission. All rights reserved.

Chapter 8—A Change of Will

1. Elisabeth Elliot, *Through Gates of Splendor* (Harper: New York, 1957).
2. C. S. Lewis, *The Problem of Pain*. (San Francisco: HarperSanFrancisco, 2001.)
3. W. Glyn Evans, *Daily with the King* (Chicago: Moody, 1989). Used by permission. All rights reserved.

Chapter 9—We Are Gifted to Serve

1. Arthur T. Pierson, quoted in J. Oswald Sanders, *The Holy Spirit and His Gifts* (Grand Rapids: Zondervan, 1970), 115.

Chapter 10—We Are Lifted to Love

1. Randy McCloy, "Rescued Miner McCloy Speaks Out for First Time," interview with Matt Lauer on MSNBC, 30 March 2006, http://www.msnbc.msn.com/id/12072995/from/RL.3. Used by permission. All rights reserved.
2. Judson Swihart, *How Do You Say "I Love You"?* (Downers Grove, IL: InterVarsity, 1977), 46-47. Used by permission. For information on this book and others by author contact him at jnswihart@kansas.net or 785-776-4105.
3. William Barclay, *The Letter to the Romans* (Philadelphia:Westminster, 1975), 164.
4. James Rowe, "Love Lifted Me," © 1912.

Chapter 14—We Are Tested by Time

1. Pat Williams, *The Warrior Within* (Ventura, CA: Regal, 2006), 151–53. Used by permission. Gospel Light/Regal books, Ventury, CA 93003.

2.   David McKinley, *The Search for Satisfaction* (Nashville: W Publishing Group, 2006).

3.   University of California, San Diego Medical Center sleep study, 29 July 2002.

4.   Bishop Ralph Cushman, "I Met God in the Morning" from *A Pocket Prayer Book* (Nashville: Abingdon Press, 1977).

5.   Charles Hummel, *The Tyranny of the Urgent* (Downers Grove, IL: InterVarsity, 1994).

Chapter 15—We Are Liberated to Live Responsibly

1.   David McKinley, *The Search for Satisfaction* (Nashville: W Publishing Group, 2006).

2.   Taken from *My Utmost for His Highest* by Oswald Chambers, © 1935 by Dodd Mead & Co., renewed © 1963 by the Oswald Chambers Publications Assn., Ltd. Used by permission of Discovery House Publishers, Grand Rapids, MI 49501. All rights reserved.

Chapter 16—We Are Strengthened to Encourage

1.   Frank Dempster Sherman, "The Joy of Friends." Used by permission.

2.   "Woman, 82, Gets Ticket for Slow Crossing," USA Today, 11 April 2006. http://www.usatoday.com/news/offbeat/2006-04-11-woman-walking_x.htm

3.   George Bernard Shaw, *Man and Superman*. (New York: Penguin, 2001).

Chapter 17—We Are Blessed to Be a Blessing

1.   Earl Woods from interview in Golf Digest, 2001.

2.   Eugene Robinson, "An Inspiring Relationship," Washington Post, 5 May 2006.

3.   Ibid.